Florida A&M University, Tallahassee
Florida Atlantic University, Boca Raton
Florida Gulf Coast University, Ft. Myers
Florida International University, Miami
Florida State University, Tallahassee
University of Central Florida, Orlando
University of Florida, Gainesville
University of North Florida, Jacksonville
University of South Florida, Tampa
University of West Florida, Pensacola

University Press of Florida

GAINESVILLE TALLAHASSEE TAMPA BOCA RATON

PENSACOLA ORLANDO MIAMI JACKSONVILLE FT. MYERS

Dolphins, Whales, and Manatees of Florida

A Guide to Sharing Their World

John E. Reynolds III and Randall S. Wells

08 07 06 05 04 03   6 5 4 3 2 1

Library of Congress Cataloging-in-Publication Data
Reynolds, John Elliott, 1952-
Dolphins, whales, and manatees of Florida: a guide to sharing
their world / John E. Reynolds III and Randall S. Wells.
p. cm.
Includes bibliographical references (p.).
ISBN 0-8130-2687-3 (p: alk. paper)
1. Dolphins—Florida. 2. Whales—Florida. 3. Manatees—Florida.
I. Wells, Randall S. II. Title.
QL737.C432R495 2003
599.5'09759—dc22   2003061689

The University Press of Florida is the scholarly publishing agency
for the State University System of Florida, comprising Florida A&M
University, Florida Atlantic University, Florida Gulf Coast University,
Florida International University, Florida State University, University
of Central Florida, University of Florida, University of North Florida,
University of South Florida, and University of West Florida.

University Press of Florida
15 Northwest 15th Street
Gainesville, FL 32611-2079
http://www.upf.com

To my long-term friends, colleagues, and mentors,
John Twiss, who has made so much difference to the world
of marine mammal conservation, and Dan Odell, who introduced
me to marine mammals and marine mammal science
in Florida a few years ago. J.E.R.

To my mentors, Ken Norris, George Rabb, and Archie Carr, for
teaching me about conservation and dedication to environmental
issues, and to my wife, Martha, for her continuing efforts to help me
learn how to communicate conservation messages effectively. R.S.W.

Contents

Acknowledgments

We are grateful to the following organizations and agencies for their support of the development of this book: the U.S. Fish and Wildlife Service (Jim Valade), and the National Marine Fisheries Service (NMFS) (Kathy Wang), now called NOAA Fisheries. Sentiel "Butch" Rommel (Florida Fish and Wildlife Conservation Commission, FWC) provided the drawings used to illustrate aspects of marine mammal anatomy. Flip Nicklin and Minden Pictures kindly provided many of the beautiful photographs used to illustrate the book. In addition, we are grateful to the following individuals and groups for allowing us to use their photographs: Florida Power & Light Company, Charles Manire, Mote Marine Laboratory's Stranding Investigations Program, New England Aquarium, Rachel Nostrom, Sheri Barton, Douglas Nowacek, Patrick Rose, and the Sirenia Project, U.S. Geological Survey.

This project was funded in part by a grant awarded from Harbor Branch Oceanographic Institution, Inc., from proceeds collected from the sale of Protect Wild Dolphins License Plate as authorized by Florida Statute 320.08058(20).

The Chicago Zoological Society provided Wells's time to participate in a number of recent research projects on human interactions with marine mammals. The FWC has provided crucial support for research investigating the behavioral responses of manatees to boat approaches. Disney Wildlife Conservation Fund, Earthwatch Institute, and the NMFS provided support for studies of dolphin responses to boat approaches. The NMFS also provided support for an evaluation of human feeding of dolphins near Sarasota, Florida. The human interaction research conducted with this support was accomplished through the superb efforts of Stephanie Nowacek, Doug Nowacek, Sue Hofmann, Kara Buckstaff, Todd Speakman, Debi Colbert, and Petra Cunningham-Smith, along with a wonderful cadre of graduate students and volunteer assistants. Mote Marine Laboratory's Stranding Investigations Program provided information from examination of dolphin carcasses. Sentiel Rommel and Tom Pitchford of the FWC Marine Mammal Pathobiology Lab provided some of the statistics on occurrence of propeller wounds on manatees.

Reynolds's work with manatees and other marine mammals in Florida has been supported by a number of agencies and organizations including Disney Wildlife Conservation Fund, Earthwatch Institute, Eckerd College, Florida Fish and Wildlife Conservation Commission, Florida Power & Light Company, Mote Marine Laboratory, National Marine Fisheries Service, Protect Wild Dolphins Program (Harbor Branch Oceanographic Institution), Reliant Energy, and U.S. Fish and Wildlife Service. He is grateful to those organizations and to his collaborators over the years.

Finally we are grateful to Kara Buckstaff, Teresa Kessenich, and the reviewers of this book (Dan Odell and Trevor Spradlin) for their helpful comments, to Ken Scott, director at the University Press of Florida, for all his assistance and flexibility, and to Gillian Hillis, project editor at the University Press of Florida, for her meticulous and careful comments on this and other books.

chapter 1

People and Marine Mammals in Florida

FOR THE PAST DECADE OR SO, something on the order of 1,000 new residents have moved to Florida every day. By the year 2030, the human population of the state may double to approximately 32 million people, with most of them occupying coastal areas. In addition, on average more than 65 million tourists have visited the state annually in recent years. The reasons for such interest in Florida are several, but clearly include the chance to experience natural resources unlike those found elsewhere in the United States. Among the resources that are near and dear to many peoples' hearts are the marine mammals.

Specifically, its diversity and abundance of marine mammals mirror Florida's general wealth of natural resources. More than two dozen species may be found in Florida's waters, including a large number of cetaceans (the group that includes whales, dolphins, and porpoises), the manatee, and even a couple of species of seals. Although people only occasionally encounter most species, some such as the manatee and the bottlenose dolphin are quite common. In some parts of the state, they are so predictably found that lucrative ecotourism ventures have developed that guarantee the opportunity to see such animals at close quarters. It is fair to say that the marine mammals play important roles not only as aesthetic and economic resources for people, but also in the integrity of Florida's coastal and riverine ecosystems.

On the other hand, the waters of Florida represent a special haven for some marine mammals that rely on those waters for their very survival as species. Florida manatees, appropriately named, cannot survive cold water and, therefore, are basically confined to the waters of that state except during those months when water temperatures north of Florida warm sufficiently to permit some animals to wander elsewhere. The right whale is the most endangered species of whale in the United States; in the North Atlantic only about 300 survivors remain, and the only known calving ground exists off the coast of northeastern Florida and southeastern Georgia.

With the steady increase in the human population of Florida, the likelihood that marine mammals and humans will encounter one another, or that marine mammals will be affected indirectly by human activities, rises steadily. Although many people cherish encounters with marine mammals and consider protection of marine mammals to be important, these species are also at the heart of some intense controversies, such as the creation of boat speed regulatory zones to protect manatees in Florida and the need for restrictions on commercial fishing to reduce marine mammal entanglement in fishing gear in other parts of the United States. We noted that people may use the presence of marine mammals for their economic advantage; however, it is also true that the presence of marine mammals may lead to economic costs or to restrictions on people. There are few more controversial groups of animals in the world today.

What Are Marine Mammals?

The marine mammals include a diverse group of animals that actually arose from different ancestors and possess very different characteristics. There are three primary groups of mammals that include marine representatives: the carnivores (represented by sea otters, marine otters, polar bears, and the diverse, flipper-footed pinnipeds [true seals, sea lions, fur seals, and walruses]), the sirenians (which include just three species of manatees and the dugong), and the cetaceans (the largest group of marine mammals, which includes all of the whales, dolphins, and porpoises). The most authoritative reference documenting all the known marine mammals is Dale Rice's *Marine Mammals of the World*, which lists

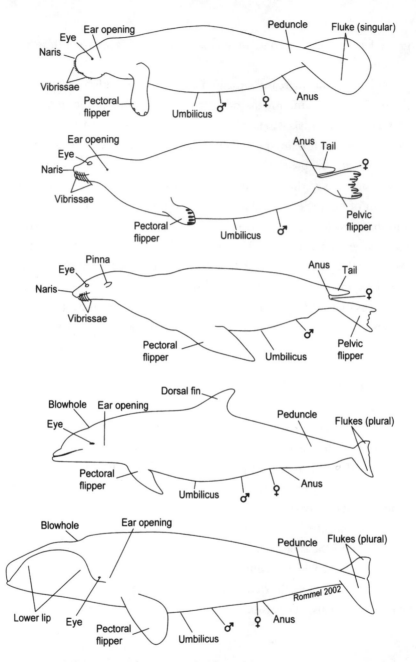

Drawings of (from top to bottom) a Florida manatee, harbor seal, California sea lion, bottlenose dolphin, and right whale illustrating their external features. Sentiel A. Rommel.

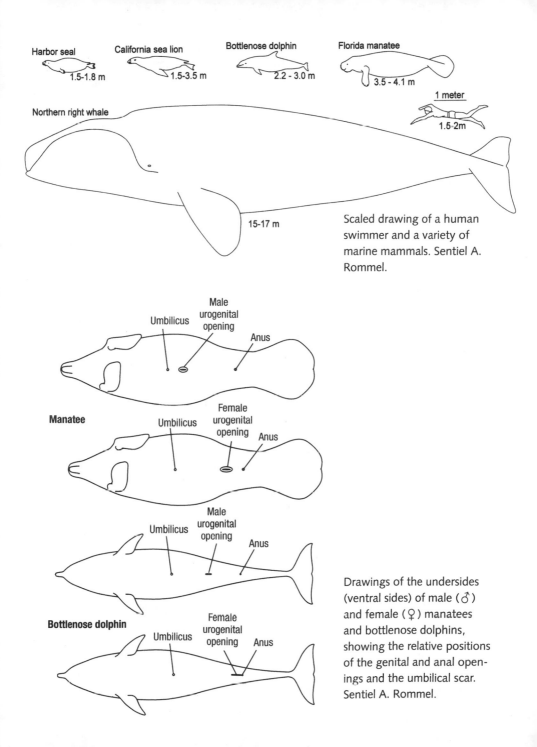

Harbor seal
1.5-1.8 m

California sea lion
1.5-3.5 m

Bottlenose dolphin
2.2 - 3.0 m

Florida manatee
3.5 - 4.1 m

1 meter
1.5-2m

Northern right whale

15-17 m

Scaled drawing of a human swimmer and a variety of marine mammals. Sentiel A. Rommel.

Manatee

Umbilicus

Male urogenital opening

Anus

Female urogenital opening

Anus

Umbilicus

Bottlenose dolphin

Umbilicus

Male urogenital opening

Anus

Female urogenital opening

Anus

Umbilicus

Drawings of the undersides (ventral sides) of male (♂) and female (♀) manatees and bottlenose dolphins, showing the relative positions of the genital and anal openings and the umbilical scar. Sentiel A. Rommel.

124 species. However, it should be recognized that many marine mammals occupy offshore, deep waters and are rarely encountered by people; thus, new species are regularly being described by scientists. In addition, new and powerful genetic techniques are allowing scientists to find that some similar-appearing animals lumped historically as a single species are actually two or more species. The number of known species of marine mammals is growing!

All of the marine mammals evolved from terrestrial mammals, and as such, they possess many traits that humans, dogs, and other "typical mammals" have, such as hair at some point in their lives, lungs, a muscular diaphragm to assist breathing, warm blood, viviparity (giving birth to live young, rather than laying eggs), and mammary glands to nourish those young. As indicated below, the ancestry of the various types of marine mammals varies considerably. Nonetheless, the marine mammals we have with us in the world today have become amazingly changed over many millions or even tens of millions of years that have elapsed since they parted ways from their terrestrial ancestors. Remarkably, the effects of natural selection have shaped the various groups of marine mammals such that they possess many features in common, including large size (an adaptation that facilitates keeping warm in an aquatic medium that draws heat from a body 25 times faster than air), streamlined body plans to permit efficient swimming and diving, and relative immobility on land.

If the various groups of marine mammals are so different from one another, it makes sense to ask why they are lumped together. The presence of some adaptations in common has been noted. There are other reasons as well: all marine mammals depend on aquatic habitats and ecosystems, making them highly visible indicators of some aspects of ecosystem health (or illness); many marine mammal populations have been seriously reduced by humans (some to the point of extinction), and conservationists perceive this to be another unifying feature; and common bases for concern about marine mammals have ultimately led to their being considered together legislatively, such as under the U.S. Marine Mammal Protection Act of 1972.

There are a number of references to which an interested reader may turn for additional information on marine mammals. Our little guide simply provides an easy-to-consult introduction. We recommend that readers interested in the general biology of marine mammals consult *Biology of Marine Mammals* (edited by John Reynolds and Sentiel Rommel) or comprehensive guidebooks such as *The Sierra Club Handbook of Whales and Dolphins* (by Stephen Leatherwood and Randall Reeves), *The Sierra Club Handbook of Seals and Sirenians* (by Reeves, Brent Stewart, and Leatherwood), *The FAO Species Identification Guide, Marine Mammals of the World* (by Tom Jefferson, Leatherwood, and Marc Webber), *National Audubon Society Guide to Marine Mammals of the World* (by Reeves, Stewart, Phillip Clapham, and James Powell), or *The Marine Mammals of the Gulf of Mexico* (by Bernd Würsig, Jefferson, and David Schmidly).

For books that provide specifics for a general audience regarding the two most common marine mammals in Florida's coastal waters we recommend *Mysterious Manatees* (by Karen Glaser and Reynolds), *Manatees and Dugongs of the World* (by Jeff Ripple), *Manatees* (by Powell), and *The Bottlenose Dolphin: Biology and Conservation* (by Reynolds, Randall Wells, and Samantha Eide). Complete citations of these and other useful references appear at the back of this book.

Cetaceans

The cetaceans are the mammals most completely adapted to an aquatic lifestyle. Cetaceans virtually never voluntarily leave the water for more than a few moments at a time. Among their most obvious features are the lack of hind limbs, which have been lost over evolutionary time, lack of hair, reduction in size of the front limbs, extremely streamlined bodies, internal reproductive organs, and the presence of powerful flukes for locomotion. Some less obvious adaptations include those associated with their sensory systems (especially their sound-producing and hearing capabilities), diving abilities (especially for some species such as the sperm whales), and the ability of most species to live in a world without fresh water. The cetaceans are most closely related to the artiodactyls, the even-toed ungulates including cows, pigs, and hippos.

The cetaceans are the most diverse and abundant marine mammals around Florida, and the most diverse, but not the most abundant group of marine mammals around the world. More than two dozen (specifically 28) species are known to occur in Florida's coastal waters or to have stranded on its beaches; 5 of those species are common and 14 others are occasionally encountered. These 19 are considered in some detail in this book.

There are two main groups of cetaceans: the mysticetes (baleen whales), characterized by features such as very large size, the presence of baleen plates rather than teeth, and two blowholes atop the head; and the odontocetes (toothed whales), which are generally smaller (except for the sperm whale), usually possess visible teeth, often are extremely social, and possess just a single blowhole. Most cetacean species are odontocetes, and all but two of Florida's cetaceans that we consider in any detail in this book are odontocetes.

Sirenians

The official State Marine Mammal of Florida is the manatee. In the video *Silent Sirens,* narrator Leonard Nimoy (Mr. Spock of *Star Trek* fame) not inaccurately calls the manatee a "bewhiskered blimp of an animal."[1] In fact, the Florida manatee is remarkably well adapted to an aquatic existence, possessing to just a slightly lesser degree most of the adaptations for an aquatic lifestyle possessed by cetaceans. But manatees have some surprising attributes, being able to dive longer than bottlenose dolphins and some other cetaceans and at times to haul their heavy bodies out on land briefly to feed or to cross mudflats. There is just one species of manatee found in Florida—the same species, but a different subspecies from that found in Caribbean waters. Manatees have occupied Florida's coastal waters for more than one million years. Despite their general similarities to whales, manatees have a very different ancestry. Their closest relatives are the elephants, and they are also related to small furry animals called hyraxes (or conies) and to aardvarks.

Carnivores

Among the various marine mammal carnivores, none is a natural, year-round resident of Florida waters. Geographically, the closest thing to a resident seal for Florida was the Caribbean monk seal, which was exterminated by people in the early 1950s. However, a couple of other pinnipeds (for example, an occasional hooded seal or harbor seal) may sometimes be found on beaches of the state, as occasional wanderers from northern waters; further, although this has not been reported for many years, in the mid- to late 1900s there were occasional reports of California sea lions that presumably escaped from zoos, oceanaria, or traveling shows.

The pinnipeds are not as completely adapted to an aquatic lifestyle as are the cetaceans and sirenians. This is reflected by the fact that pinnipeds have retained all four limbs possessed by their ancestors, most species have fur, which can be extremely dense, and they regularly come out on land or ice, where they have relatively good mobility, to give birth, mate, molt, or rest. Nonetheless, the pinnipeds possess streamlined bodies that can slice through the water very quickly, and some species, such as elephant seals, rank among the world's best divers, able to submerge for well over an hour and to depths of a mile or so.

All of the carnivorous marine mammals are descended from terrestrial carnivores such as bears and weasels.

Why Do People Care about Marine Mammals?

In the 1960s, whales and dolphins came, for some people, to symbolize the beauty and freedom of the seas. From the ancient Greeks through the present time, marine mammals have somehow claimed a special place in peoples' minds and lore.[2]

There are many reasons people seem to care about marine mammals. These include aesthetic appreciation for their beauty, majesty, or cuteness; the sense of kinship to animals such as bottlenose dolphins that are considered by some people to be "intelligent"; concern for the health of aquatic ecosystems that support both marine mammals and many human enterprises; the many ways in which humans can or do benefit from the presence of marine mammals, including but not limited to economic gain and benefits of physiological or biomedical research; and a feeling of stewardship. A remarkably good discussion of reasons people should value manatees (and by extension all marine mammals, and even all species) was written several years ago by Daryl Domning, titled "Why Save the Manatee?"

However, it must be recognized that some people care about marine mammals because the animals may cost them time and money and may cause certain restrictions or regulations of human activities. Some fishermen, for example, consider marine mammals to be extremely effective (and unwelcome!) competitors for resources. In some places in the world, marine mammals frequently become entangled in nets and other gear, damaging that gear and creating delays that frustrate fishermen, not to mention causing serious jeopardy for the marine mammals themselves. As noted above, boat speed regulations to protect endangered manatees cause delays and create frustration among recreational and commercial users of certain waterways.

Primarily because of their potential economic impacts, marine mammals receive a lot of attention in Florida, just as they do elsewhere around the world. As noted by Reynolds in *Mysterious Manatees* and elsewhere, people with different values and opinions about conservation of marine mammals need to communicate better and more often to seek points of common ground and to create a future that balances human wishes and needs with the survival needs of living marine resources such as the marine mammals.

Marine mammals have tended to polarize peoples' views. For some, the marine mammals symbolize a pristine natural world, whereas for others marine mammals represent impediments to making a living or simply to recreation. For readers interested in a range of issues revolving around marine mammals, especially those in the United States, we recommend various chapters contained in *Conservation and Management of Marine Mammals* (edited by John Twiss and Randall Reeves).

Why Does This Book Exist?

We have spent much of our lives in Florida and much of our professional lives studying or working to conserve marine mammals. Like many or most Floridians, we value our time on the water, be it spent fishing, traveling, or simply drifting and relaxing. And like some Floridians, our business (i.e., marine research) depends on our regular use of Florida's waterways. We are also concerned about the growth of Florida's human population and about the cumulative effects of so many people on finite spaces and species.

A lot has been made in the popular presses about how "special" marine mammals are. Our goal is NOT to reinforce the "dolphin-hugger" mentality; in fact it is quite the opposite. But we suggest that marine mammals are, in fact, special. As long-lived, slow breeding mammals with very specialized biological needs, they are extremely easy to impact. Where a population of mosquitoes, mice, or mullet can grow rapidly and reoccupy an affected habitat, marine mammal populations are biologically constrained and can recover only very slowly. If people want to keep marine mammals around, a conservative approach to the animals' management and to maintaining their habitat is a must.

This book has been written for two primary purposes: (1) to inform people about the marine mammals they see in the wild, and (2) to discuss enjoyable ways in which people can interact with free-ranging marine mammals while minimizing the harm such interactions can inadvertently cause. We have attempted to create a reasonably comprehensive little book that can easily be taken into the field where it can serve as a resource to people as they encounter and interact with marine mammals. We hope that readers of our book will help create and perpetuate standards for encountering marine mammals that will allow people in the future to share the enjoyment of such interactions. Ultimately, we seek to promote a balance whereby people can continue to do activities they enjoy at the same time that the health and well-being of marine mammals are not compromised.

The evolution of human attitudes in North America regarding marine mammals has been summarized nicely in a chapter by David Lavigne, Victor Scheffer, and Steve Kellert (see Twiss and Reeves). In it, the authors suggest[3] that currently we may be in the midst of "a time when the conservation gains of the twentieth century began to erode, ostensibly to facilitate economic growth and development." In fact, they suggest that the twentieth century may retrospectively be viewed "as an anomaly, a time when people tried, for a while at least, to reduce their impacts on wild populations and their habitats, and, to their own detriment, ultimately failed." We hope that this pessimistic perspective may turn out to be wrong and that some of the ideas we develop in this book help serve in some small way as an antidote.

chapter 2

Natural History of
Florida's Marine Mammals

THIS CHAPTER PROVIDES an introduction to some species of marine mammals that are encountered commonly or occasionally in Florida's waterways or on its beaches; we also simply list some of the very rare occupants. Our intention is to provide readers with some background information so that they may appreciate how these animals behave and "earn their living." Such information at hand may facilitate understanding of how human activities can affect marine mammal activities in detrimental ways.

Scientific names for species sometimes vary among authors. Except in a few cases where a different common usage prevails (for example, northern right whale), we have used the nomenclature endorsed in Dale Rice's *Marine Mammals of the World*.

We have tried to provide minimum population estimates for each of the species described below, as provided in National Oceanic and Atmospheric Administration (NOAA) Stock Assessment Reports produced each year. The quality of these estimates varies with the species and habitat. In some cases, such as northern right whales, estimates are counts of identifiable individuals because the population has been reduced to a few hundred individuals. In other cases, estimates are calculated from density estimates developed from aerial or shipboard surveys.

Commonly Encountered Marine Mammals

Florida Manatee (*Trichechus manatus latirostris*)

Physical Description: The Florida manatee is the largest living sirenian, with adults routinely exceeding 10 feet (3 m) in length and a ton (2,000 pounds; 900 kg) in weight. Exceptionally large individuals may exceed 13 feet (approximately 4 m) and 3,500 pounds (nearly 1,600 kg). Newborn

One of Florida's most common marine mammals, the Florida manatee. The object tethered to the manatee is a radio tag used by scientists to track manatees. Rachel Nostrom.

A mother manatee and her calf. Patrick M. Rose, Save the Manatee Club.

manatees average about 4 feet (1.2 m) long and weigh more than 60 pounds (27 kg), but they grow quickly, sometimes reaching lengths in excess of 8 feet (nearly 2.5 m) and weights over 550 pounds (250 kg) before they reach three years of age.

Manatees are streamlined, but to a lesser degree than is the case with most cetaceans. Over the surface of the body, there are very sparse hairs that may serve a sensory function, such as detecting pressure waves created by manatees swimming nearby. Hairs in the form of whiskers (vibrissae) are more abundant around the mouth. The faces of manatees are rather bulbous, with large, flexible, and muscular lips that maneuver food into the mouth. Manatees possess molar-like teeth that become worn down by the gritty vegetation they consume; however, the worn teeth are lost and are methodically replaced by new teeth throughout the life of the animal.

Paired nostrils, which are closed by valve-like flaps, lie at the end of the head. The front (pectoral) flippers are flexible, with obvious nails at the tips. The fluke, which can propel the animals at reasonably high speeds (perhaps 20 mph [32 kph] for short bursts) is rounded and extremely powerful. The reproductive organs of manatees are internal, and nipples are located in the "arm pits" of females.

Distribution and Ranging Patterns: Florida manatees are found year-round in coastal and riverine waters of peninsular Florida. When water temperatures warm in the spring and summer, some manatees wander nomadically and are regularly spotted in Georgia and the Carolinas. In the northern Gulf of Mexico, manatees appear in coastal waters of Alabama, Mississippi, Louisiana, and Texas in summer. Occasionally, manatees wander even farther: "Chessie," for example, traveled as far as Rhode Island and back in summer 1996, and rare individuals even travel from Florida to the Bahamas. Manatees appear to exist equally well in freshwater, marine, and estuarine environments.

Abundance: This topic is hotly debated. Manatees are extremely difficult to census because of their wide distribution and tendency to occupy waters with limited visibility. It is likely that an accurate and precise count of manatees is unattainable. Many scientists believe that approximately 3,500 manatees occupy Florida's waters at the turn of the twenty-first century, with roughly equal numbers on the east and west coasts.

Most scientists would agree that understanding trends in manatee abundance is probably more important for conservation and management than a single precise count. Managers and scientists consider that there are four so-called subpopulations of manatees in Florida: a northwestern population, a southwestern population, a population located in the upper St. Johns River, and an Atlantic coast population. The north-western and upper St. Johns River subpopulations are believed to be growing well, but together, they constitute only about 16 percent of the total manatee population for the state. The Atlantic coast subpopulation is the largest (containing approximately 47 percent of Florida's manatees) and there is evidence that this subpopulation is either stable or perhaps even slightly increasing in recent years. The southwestern subpopulation is the least well studied, and population trends are poorly documented. However, recent studies and analyses have suggested that the subpopulation in the southwest is, at best, stable, and is possibly in decline.

Social and Other Behavior: Manatees are frequently observed as solitary individuals or as members of small groups. This stands in contrast to some of the very large herds that exist for certain species of cetaceans (see spinner and spotted dolphins, for example). The frequency with which manatees are observed alone or in small groups has sometimes led to the erroneous belief that manatees are fundamentally asocial.

Manatee society has also been described as "ephemeral," meaning that there is no core, long-term social unit; rather, animals tend to drift into and out of groups. Nonetheless, there is increasing evidence that manatees appear to spend more time with some individuals in an area than others.

The longest and closest social bond is that between a mother manatee and her calf (or calves—twins occur a little more than 1 percent of the time). Even though a calf may be nutritionally dependent on its mother for only a few months, calves typically remain with their mothers for a year or longer. It is thought that mothers "teach" their offspring[1] important aspects of habitat use: where warm-water discharges exist and when to seek them; where abundant food resources exist; and where freshwater sources lie.

A tagged manatee named Beau basks in the warm waters of Crystal River. U.S. Geological Survey, Florida Integrated Science Center, Sirenia Project.

Another social entity in manatees is the so-called mating herd, a group comprising a female manatee in estrus and a consort of up to a dozen and a half males that attempt to mate with her. Mating herds are characterized by a lot of physical activity as males jockey for position near the female or she tries to avoid their amorous intentions, often by swimming into shallow water. Mating herds may last for a few weeks.

When winter weather turns cold, many manatees seek warm water in natural springs (such as Crystal River or Blue Spring in northern Florida) or in the discharges of power plants (warm-water effluent from power plants is typically clean water warmed in the process of cooling equipment associated with electricity generation). Some of these groups may contain more than 500 individuals. However, scientists do not consider them to be social groups. Instead, they are considered as "aggregations" that form as the result of a common response by the animals to an environmental stimulus (in this case, cold weather), rather than for social reasons.

Food and Feeding: Manatees in Florida consume a wide variety of plants, ranging from algae to mangrove seedlings, sea grasses, and freshwater grasses. They consume plants growing on the bottom, in the water

To escape winter's cold, manatees may aggregate in huge numbers at natural springs and in the discharges of power plants, such as the one pictured here at Riviera Beach. John E. Reynolds and Florida Power & Light Company.

column, and at the surface. In addition, manatees occasionally haul their bodies partially out of the water to consume plants growing on the bank. It has been said (only half jokingly) that if something is green and cannot swim fast, manatees will eat it! In reality there are a few plants that manatees seem not to eat. Blue-green algae, for example, can contain toxins, and manatees appear to avoid eating them.

Manatees have a digestive system generally like that of a horse. In such a system, the large intestine is greatly expanded as a chamber in which microbes break down cellulose (the material contained in plant cell walls); this relationship with the microbes is necessary because mammals lack the digestive enzymes to efficiently break down plant materials for optimal nutrition. The microbial activity in the enlarged large intestine (or hindgut) may also be the source of considerable heat that helps manatees stay warm in winter. The large intestine alone in a Florida manatee can measure more than 66 feet (20 m) long (compared with less than 3 feet [1 m] in humans) and weigh more than 250 pounds (113 kg)—it is truly enlarged!!

Hindgut digesters need to eat much of the day, in contrast to the ruminants such as cows and sheep, which have a more efficient digestive system, with enlarged, multiple stomachs as the sites of cellulose breakdown. Manatees, in fact, may eat for six to eight hours each day and consume 100–200 pounds (45–90 kg) of vegetation in that time. They use their flexible front limbs and their prehensile, muscular lips to maneuver food into the mouth.

There has been concern among some people about the possibility that in areas where manatees are abundant, their grazing might be injurious to the health of sea grass beds, and thereby affect local productivity. In reality, grazing by herbivores can sometimes lead to better productivity and plant species diversity. Consider your own lawn—it grows much faster if you mow it than if you do not.

Nearly 100 manatees are struck by motorboats and killed each year. An unknown number are struck and seriously injured, but not killed. The long-term effects of collisions with boats are not clear but may include impairment of immune system function and reproductive ability. U.S. Geological Survey, Florida Integrated Science Center, Sirenia Project.

As noted above, manatees can swim quickly (more than 20 mph) in short bursts, but they generally cruise slowly through the water. Although manatees are not deep divers, they can remain submerged when resting for more than 20 minutes.

Mortality Factors and Threats: Because of an effective carcass salvage network that has functioned since 1974, scientists know a great deal about what kills manatees. In recent years, an average of nearly one dead manatee per day is recovered and examined by scientists. The agency responsible for this work today and in the recent past is the Florida Fish and Wildlife Conservation Commission.

More than 4,000 carcasses have been examined to date. Growth layers in the ear bones allow scientists to determine an animal's age. The animals that have been recovered are as old as 59 years, although most do not live nearly that long. The average age of the manatees recovered and aged to date is seven.

Approximately 25–30 percent of all deaths of manatees occur as a result of collisions with watercraft. Death due to cuts inflicted by propellers occurs in about 50 percent of the cases and due simply to the impact of the boat or ship in the other half of the cases. One dead manatee had scars that suggested it had been struck on 50 separate occasions in its life. One should bear in mind that most adult manatees have been struck by boats at some point in their lives; although these events certainly involve considerable pain for the manatees, scientists do not know the extent to which single or multiple collisions impair reproductive performance, immune function, or other necessary biological activities.

Other human related causes of death include crushing in flood control structures (dam gates) or canal locks, entanglement in or ingestion of fishing gear, and occasional vandalism. Thus, although collisions with watercraft kill more manatees than does any other identifiable cause, human activities that impact manatees are not confined to boating.

Two important natural causes of death include exposure to cold in winter and exposure to red tide toxin (called brevetoxin). It is worth noting that some scientists believe that human activities may influence the frequency or intensity of red tides. In addition, the presence of warm-water discharges at power plants in northern Florida may influence the number of manatees exposed to cold water in winter, especially if the power plant shuts down for a period of time during a cold spell and ceases discharging warm water. Thus, human activities may be affecting the extent of "natural mortality" in manatees.

Cause of death for one-third of the recovered carcasses is officially listed as undetermined. In addition, 20–25 percent of the animals recovered are young calves (categorized as perinatal animals) for which cause of death is uncertain. Therefore, it is accurate to state that cause of death is not known for more than half of the carcasses that are examined. This may seem surprisingly high, but it reflects both the rate at which carcasses decompose in Florida's warm and humid climate and the general state of knowledge about marine mammal pathology. In fact, the state laboratory that conducts the necropsies has received extensive praise from knowledgeable pathologists and zoologists for the quantity and quality of information it is able to extract from these carcasses and incorporate into a long-term database.

In Florida, there are no known natural predators on manatees. But there are threats other than those that directly kill manatees. We have mentioned that manatees are vulnerable to cold winter weather. That susceptibility may soon present an enormous problem for manatees. With the advent of new, cheaper means by which to produce electricity, it is probable that some of the power plants on which manatees depend for warm water in winter may cease to function in the near future. Within a few decades, power production as we know it today will have disappeared—and with it, important sources of warm water for manatees.

Equally alarming is that human use of the underground aquifer in Florida, along with some recent droughts, has lessened the flow of warm water at important natural warm-water discharges such as Blue Spring in northeastern Florida. Biologists fear that soon even major natural springs may no longer produce enough warm water to protect manatees during cold winter weather. Sadly, scientists and managers have produced few viable options for the care of manatees when they become quite literally "left out in the cold." Only the Florida Power & Light Company has, to date, provided specific recommendations for development of new, nonindustrial, sustainable warm-water sources in areas used by manatees in winter.

When manatees lose their sources of warm water in winter, some animals may not know to move south to warmer water, and they may perish. Others that migrate south may become tightly packed in the southern parts of Florida for longer periods of time than is the case today. It is possible that they may overgraze their food resources, which may affect health and reproduction. In addition, the survivors will spend more time in waters that are completely urbanized and heavily traveled by watercraft. The latter factor may lead, as discussed earlier, to higher levels of mortality and serious injury. Being in close proximity to high numbers of boats may also stress manatees because of noise and physical disturbance; we don't know what the effects of chronic, high stress might be on manatees, but we do know that it is not beneficial to humans and some other mammals.

The issue of the effects that unabated physical disturbance might have on wildlife is discussed in chapter 4. However, we should recognize that the human species may precipitate stresses in wildlife in a number of accidental ways: through the introduction of high noise levels from boats, aircraft, bridges, and dredge and fill; through thousands of people swimming at natural springs in winter to obtain a close-up view of manatees that are only trying to avoid the effects of murderous cold; or through driving high-speed boats near manatees.

One additional threat needs to be mentioned as well. First, as the aquifer gets tapped to meet the growing demands of a burgeoning human population, not only will warm water in winter disappear, but so may easy and widespread access to freshwater for manatees to drink. In some locations, desalination plants will render freshwater for people and in the process make inshore waters saltier. Over the long term, it is likely that a number of marine and estuarine plants (not just marine mammals) may be affected by ecological changes caused by our population growth and its requirements for freshwater. Particularly problematic for Florida's water resources are the exacerbating effects of urban sprawl and the inadequacy of planning to deal with human population growth.[2] Lack of freshwater will doubtless be one of the greatest ecological issues facing the Sunshine State in the decades to come.

Bottlenose Dolphin (*Tursiops truncatus*)

Physical Description: The bottlenose dolphin is the "quintessential dolphin" in many peoples' minds because it is frequently seen in near-shore waters, and is the most common dolphin in oceanarium displays, movies, and television.[3] The "bottlenose" in the name refers to the dolphin's short, robust, cylindrical beak (rostrum). The beak contains about 20–25 cone-shaped teeth in each upper and lower jaw. These counter-shaded dolphins are generally dark gray dorsally, grading through shades of gray on the sides, to white on the belly. Bottlenose dolphins are medium-sized dolphins. Adult coastal bottlenose dolphins range up to 9.5 feet (2.9 m) in length, and up to about 600 pounds (280 kg) in weight. Adult males are slightly longer and heavier than females. Bottlenose dolphin dorsal fins tend to be tall and falcate (recurved), and the pectoral flippers are longer

The charismatic and acrobatic bottlenose dolphin is frequently seen in coastal waters of Florida. Randall S. Wells.

and broader than those of many other dolphins. The flukes are slightly overlapping. A variation of the bottlenose dolphin found in deep, offshore waters of Florida and elsewhere tends to be larger and darker in color, with a longer and more slender tailstock (peduncle).

In Florida, females generally reach sexual maturity at 5–10 years of age, at a body length of at least 7.2 feet (220 cm), and after a 12-month gestation period they produce a single calf every three to six years. The calf is nursed from nipples on each side of the genital slit. Reproduction continues into the late forties. In western Florida, where the most complete data on age structure are available, the oldest free-ranging females documented to date have been 53 years old, but few individuals attain this extreme age. Males reach sexual maturity at about 10 years of age, at a body length of at least 8 feet (245 cm), and a few individuals may live into their mid-forties.

Distribution and Ranging Patterns: Bottlenose dolphins are found in temperate, subtropical, and tropical waters throughout the world, from near the equator to the Moray Firth of Scotland. Dolphins in geographically dispersed locations may differ greatly in size, coloration, numbers of teeth, and other features. Recent genetic studies suggest these variations may be associated with the existence of more species of bottlenose dolphins than the two that are currently recognized by most scientists (including the Indian Ocean bottlenose dolphin, *Tursiops aduncus*).

Bottlenose dolphins occur in most of the available marine habitats in Florida waters, with the exception of waters more than 3,000 feet (1,000 m) deep. They are abundant in bays, sounds, and estuaries, and along open shorelines, and they can be found over the continental shelf, and on the shelf edge and slope. At times, they swim through waters less than 3 feet (1 m) deep, and may even beach themselves very briefly to capture prey fish. They are also known to swim into rivers.

Bottlenose dolphins demonstrate a variety of ranging patterns, as scientists have learned from tagging dolphins, tracking them, and repeatedly observing identifiable dolphins with distinctive natural markings on their dorsal (back) fins. Ranging patterns vary from long-term, year-round residents of particular bays, to seasonal migrants, with a variety of intermediate patterns occurring as well. Seasonal migrations are known for bottlenose dolphins along the mid-Atlantic seaboard, but have not yet been clearly documented for Florida dolphins. Little is known about the ranging patterns of dolphins living outside of the bays, sounds, and estuaries, except that the ranges are large, extending beyond the limits of the studies conducted to date.

Two young male dolphins, Misha and Echo, that were captured in Tampa Bay, briefly held in captivity, and released to assess their ability to become re-integrated into dolphin society. Randall S. Wells.

Bays, sounds, and estuaries often form all or part of the ranges of coastal dolphins. Some dolphins may use several different bay systems, connected by open waters, over periods of months or years. More commonly, dolphins occupying bays spend most of their time in those enclosed areas and the immediately surrounding waters. In Florida, multi-year residency has been reported for dolphins living in Choctawhatchee Bay in the panhandle, Cedar Keys, Boca Ciega Bay, Tampa Bay, Sarasota Bay, Lemon Bay, Charlotte Harbor, Pine Island Sound, Estero Bay, Biscayne Bay, the Indian and Banana Rivers, and waters associated with the mouth of the St. John's River near Jacksonville.

Arguably the best-studied group of resident dolphins in the world lives in Sarasota Bay, Florida, where they have been under study since 1970. Currently, about 140 dolphins inhabit a 30,887-acre (125 square km; 48 square mile) home range, including Sarasota Bay. The residents comprise at least four generations of identifiable individuals. This group is not a "population" in the strictest sense of the word because there is genetic exchange with other population units. It is referred to as a "community" because the animals share a home range and associate with each other more than they associate with dolphins in adjacent waters. These dolphins are observed year-round in the area, but use the habitat differently depending on season. During warm months many of the residents spend much of their time in the shallow bays, near sea grass meadows. During colder months, they spend more time in channels, in passes between barrier islands, and along the adjacent Gulf of Mexico shoreline. Dolphins born to community residents typically remain in the area. Occasionally, new dolphins immigrate into the community range, on either a seasonal or permanent basis. Resident males may leave the home range for periods of time, presumably to breed with females outside of the community. Comparable communities have been identified in Tampa Bay and Charlotte Harbor, forming a mosaic of community home ranges along the central west coast of Florida.

Abundance: NOAA Fisheries (previously called the National Marine Fisheries Service), the agency within the U.S. Department of Commerce tasked with assessing and protecting populations of marine mammals, estimates that at least 67,000 bottlenose dolphins reside in the Gulf of Mexico, including approximately 4,000 living in bays, sounds, and estuaries.[4] No good estimates exist for the numbers of dolphins along the east coast of Florida. The species is protected under the Federal Marine Mammal Protection Act, but it is not considered to be endangered anywhere in U.S. waters. Much controversy currently exists regarding a congressional designation of the "coastal migratory stock" of bottlenose dolphins along the mid-Atlantic region of the United States as "depleted" following the deaths of at least 750 dolphins during 1987–88. Many of these dolphins were believed to have died from a morbillivirus, a type of distemper virus. The exact number of animals that died, past and current abundance of dolphins, and extent to which one or more stocks (management units) of dolphins were involved in and affected by the die-off are all unknown at this time. The degree to which Florida bottlenose dolphins were impacted by this event remains to be evaluated once revision of stock identifications along the Atlantic seaboard is complete.

Social and Other Behavior: Some of the first indications of the behavioral and social complexities of bottlenose dolphins resulted from observations of small colonies of dolphins in oceanarium settings beginning in the late 1930s. Social interactions were frequent, involving both agonistic (aggressive, including biting, ramming, tail slaps, etc.) and affiliative (bonding or acceptance, including stroking, rubbing, and sexual) behaviors within the framework of a dominance hierarchy based on gender, age, and size, with adult males dominant over all other pool-mates.

Bottlenose dolphins in oceanaria exhibit a large repertoire of behaviors, many of which have been subsequently shaped by trainers into the displays of abilities presented to the public at many dolphin shows. The animals have demonstrated a keen ability to solve problems presented to them in experimental trials as well as during everyday life in the pool. Their cognitive skills—including their ability to process information—are further reflected by the rapidity and effectiveness with which they are able to acquire and perfect trained behaviors.

In addition to highly advanced learning and problem solving abilities, the dolphins' cognitive abilities involve extensive use of a variety of sounds. Bottlenose dolphins produce three basic categories of sounds: pure tone whistles, squawks known as "burst pulses," and echolocation or sonar "clicks." Each dolphin has a large repertoire of whistles that it produces, but it tends to produce one whistle more often than any other— this is known as its "signature whistle." Results of studies in pools and in the wild suggest that signature whistles are used as identifiers for individuals, and may facilitate maintaining contact across dolphin schools when underwater visibility is limiting. Burst pulses occur most frequently in social situations, where dolphins are actively interacting with one another—rubbing, chasing, biting, copulating, etc. The dolphin's sonar system involves the production in the dolphin head of clicks that are projected forward in a very narrow beam. The clicks bounce off reflective objects in their environment, and the echoes are received through the dolphins' lower jaws, thereby helping the animal to navigate, locate prey, and avoid threats. This system remains the envy of human engineers because of the dolphins' ability to make very fine discriminations between objects and materials. Commonly held beliefs that bottlenose dolphins are constantly using their echolocation in the wild have been found to be incorrect—they apparently use the system as necessary, which tends to be infrequently. Passive listening may provide the animals with much information about their acoustically rich environment (including allowing them to approach some noisy prey fish without having to announce their approach through echolocation).

Field studies since the early 1970s have begun to place the behaviors of these animals into perspective relative to the ecological pressures that have shaped them over the millennia. Over the last 30 years, scores of research projects have been conducted at many locations through the species range of bottlenose dolphins, greatly enhancing our understanding of the dolphins' biology and behavior.

Most sightings of wild dolphins involve first seeing the animals' dorsal fins when they surface to breathe. In the shallow inshore waters of the central west coast of Florida, bottlenose dolphins typically surface about twice each minute, on average, though dives of more than 4.5 minutes have been recorded on rare occasion. Not surprisingly, the average dive durations for dolphins inhabiting deeper waters farther offshore tend to be longer, about one to two minutes or more. The deeper-water dolphins have an increased capacity for storing oxygen in their blood.

Dolphins are "voluntary breathers," meaning that they must remain conscious to breathe. Thus, it is thought by some scientists that dolphins employ a novel method for sleeping, by resting one half of their brain at a time and reducing their overall activity level, but remaining sufficiently "conscious" to breathe and carry on basic survival behaviors.

The swimming speeds of bottlenose dolphins typically average about 2–4 miles per hour (approximately 3–6 km per hour), though they are capable of brief bursts of speed in excess of 20 miles per hour (30 km per hour). Radio-tracking studies have shown that the animals are on the move throughout the day and night.

Bottlenose dolphins occasionally "surf" the bow wave or the stern wake of vessels, or breaking waves near shore or over sandbars. The calf learns to ride pressure waves during its first few days of life, when its mother begins to use "assisted locomotion" to keep the calf alongside without large expenditures of the calf's energy. The calf rides close to the mother's dorsal fin, being pulled along in the mother's pressure wave. In this way the calf moves at the same speed as its mother for minutes on end, without having to beat its own flukes.

Dolphin activities in the wild follow a pattern of alternating "bouts." The basic categories of activities recorded by a number of behavioral researchers include:

1. *feeding,* when a fish is noted in a dolphin's mouth or a dolphin is seen obviously chasing prey;

2. *traveling,* when the dolphins move steadily in one direction;

3. *milling,* when the dolphins move in a variety of directions in a single location;

4. *socializing,* when two or more dolphins interact with one another, often involving such behaviors as leaps of many kinds, tail slaps, explosive exhalations known as "chuffs," and all kinds of physical contact;

5. *playing,* when a dolphin interacts with an object; and

6. *resting,* when the animals surface slowly and relatively synchronously and are not obviously engaged in any other activities.

Typically one or two kinds of activity predominate for a period of time, and then the group shifts to another activity. For example, feeding dolphins may converge and begin to travel after several minutes. Within a mile or two they may begin to engage in socializing, followed by more traveling and then perhaps by feeding or resting.

Bottlenose dolphins tend to be social animals. Over the species' range, they can be found in groups of up to 100 or so individuals. In the inshore waters of Florida, bottlenose dolphins may occur in groups of up to 20–30 individuals or more, but smaller groups of four to seven are more common, and individuals are sometimes seen alone. Contrary to popular beliefs that bottlenose dolphins occur in stable "pods" or in human-like families, groups in inshore waters tend to be fluid in composition, exhibiting a pattern described above for manatees as "fission-fusion." Individuals seen together early in the day may be seen associating with a different set of animals within a few hours. Along the central west coast of

Florida, groups have been found to have the following three basic components:

1. *nursery groups,* of females with their most recent calves;

2. *juvenile groups,* including young dolphins of both genders up to their mid-teens; and

3. *adult males,* as single individuals or, more commonly, as members of strongly bonded pairs.

Observed groups are typically combinations of one or more of these basic units. Nursery groups tend to be the largest groups seen, and often are formed around females with calves of similar age, regardless of kin relationships. Specific group composition may change frequently. Calves typically remain with their mothers for three to six years, well beyond weaning. Older female offspring may swim with, and "baby-sit" for, their mothers following the birth of subsequent siblings—this may provide opportunities for them to learn how to rear calves of their own.

Juvenile groups tend to be intermediate in size, and often provide the most entertainment to observers because of the frequent bouts of socializing and play in which they engage.

As males reach sexual maturity, they begin to form pair bonds with other males of similar age and often with similar "childhood backgrounds." Once pairs are formed (and more than 80 percent of males form pairs at some time in their life), they remain intact for the lives of the males. If one member dies, often the remaining partner attempts to develop a pair bond with another male. It is believed that these pairings may improve feeding efficiency, provide protection, and even yield enhanced reproductive opportunities. Paternity tests of Sarasota Bay dolphins conducted by Debbie Duffield of Portland State University have shown that bottlenose dolphins are not monogamous—females may use different males to father subsequent calves. Both single and paired males, ranging in age from 13 to 40 years, have been identified as probable fathers, but paired males are more likely to be sires than are unpaired males. Fathers do not appear to participate in the rearing of calves.

A special case of social behavior engaged in by bottlenose and other dolphins is "epimeletic" or caregiving behavior. This involves dolphins providing aid or physical support to sick or injured individuals, holding them at the surface, or protecting them from threats. Most commonly, this behavior takes the form of mothers continuing to support their newborn calves even after the calves have died. Epimeletic behavior may be the basis for the occasional instances when humans report having been rescued by dolphins.

Food and Feeding: The list of prey items consumed by bottlenose dolphins is quite lengthy, and varies from location to location. Inshore dolphins feed primarily on fish, while more open water dolphins may also feed upon squid. Other invertebrates may also appear in stomach contents on occasion. Bottlenose dolphins tend to capture single prey items, typically 2–12 inches (5–30 cm) in length. Depending on the dolphin's size and whether it is lactating, a single dolphin may eat 10–35 pounds (about 5–15 kg) of fish and/or squid each day.

Along Florida's central west coast, bottlenose dolphins feed primarily on pinfish, pigfish (a type of croaker), spot, and mullet. The primary habitat of these fish includes sea grass meadows. All four species make sounds that are audible to dolphins, prompting the suggestion from several researchers that the dolphins may be selecting them at least in part because they can locate them without having to use echolocation.

Dolphins employ a variety of behaviors to capture prey. Typically, individual dolphins catch individual prey on their own, but they can also engage in coordinated, cooperative feeding with other dolphins at times when feeding on schooling prey. Dolphins in Florida waters demonstrate several curious feeding patterns. "Fishwhacking" is a shallow-water behavior in which a dolphin slaps a fish with either the dorsal or ventral side of its flukes, often launching a stunned fish into the air. "Kerplunking" is another shallow-water behavior, in which the dolphin drives its tail stock and flukes vertically through the water's surface, creating a noisy geyser of spray as well as a cavitation and bubble stream below the surface, presumably trying to flush prey from hiding places. In areas where tidal creeks and emergent vegetation occur, dolphins may drive prey onto the mud banks and actually slide out of the water to grab these prey before sliding back into the water. In other areas such as the Florida Keys, bottlenose dolphins may create mud plumes that apparently serve as a barrier to some fish.

The sharp, interdigitating teeth of the upper and lower jaws allow the dolphin to grasp prey, while the tongue maneuvers the prey to pass down the dolphin's throat headfirst. Individual prey items are usually consumed intact—the arrangement of dolphin teeth and jaws is not conducive to chewing. However, some prey species require special handling, because of size or other features. Dolphins can break up large prey by rubbing them on the bottom or shaking them in air. Fish with dangerous or painful spines, such as catfish, can also be consumed after separating the desirable from the undesirable parts of the fish. Bottlenose dolphins have been observed to remove the tails from catfish, leaving the tailless heads, complete with pectoral and dorsal spines, swimming until they bleed out.

Mortality Factors and Threats: Bottlenose dolphins suffer from a variety of threats, both natural and of human origin (anthropogenic). Mortality rates are difficult to measure in the wild—they require knowledge of the community to know which or how many individuals are missing, or to know that carcasses recovered on the beach are from the local com-

Propeller wounds on a bottlenose dolphin near Sarasota, Florida. Randall S. Wells.

munity. Few communities are known this completely, but the Sarasota Bay dolphins provide one source of information in this regard. On average, about 4–5 percent of the dolphins are lost each year. This proportion probably includes mostly deaths, and about half of the missing dolphins are recovered as carcasses, but in the absence of a carcass it is often not possible to distinguish between death and emigration (permanent movement out of the area).

Natural mortality includes losses from disease, injury, predation, and the failure of young calves to thrive. The only known predators of bottlenose dolphins in Florida waters are large sharks, such as bull, tiger, and dusky sharks. Shark bite scars are found on about 31 percent of Sarasota Bay dolphins. Given the relatively small number of shark bite scars acquired by individuals over periods of several decades or more, shark bite scars likely reflect a rare agonistic encounter that the dolphin survived. Sharks are probably a greater threat to small dolphins than large ones, because more of the small individual fits into a shark's mouth. However, shark predation may not be nearly as important today as it was 30 to 40 years ago because of tremendous reductions in shark populations through overfishing. Scientists at Mote Marine Laboratory in Sarasota, Florida, estimate that populations of large sharks may have been reduced by 80 percent. Of greater concern today are stingrays, as barbs from these fish account for an increasing number of deaths and injuries to dolphins. Rather than indicating an increasing tendency toward aggressiveness on the part of stingrays, this change probably reflects increases in stingray numbers as their primary predators, large sharks, have declined. In fact, bottlenose dolphins are occasionally seen flipping or "playing with" small rays, a behavior that may create an opportunity for the dolphin to become seriously injured.

Anthropogenic factors currently affecting bottlenose dolphins in Florida waters include: entanglement in fishing gear, ingestion of fishing gear, boat traffic, coastal development, direct human interactions, and environmental contaminants. Dolphins in Florida waters die or are seriously injured from being entangled in a variety of fishing gears, including commercial fishing nets, recreational fishing gear including monofilament line and terminal tackle (hooks, lures), and crab trap float lines. About 11 percent of dolphins in Sarasota Bay bear entanglement scars; most were apparently acquired while the animals were young. Since the mid-1990s, commercial fishing nets have ceased being a major factor in dolphin mortality in inshore waters, as large gill nets were banned from inshore waters by a Florida state constitutional amendment. Of greater concern in inshore locations today is recreational fishing gear. Dolphins, especially calves, become entangled in fishing line stripped off reels and discarded into the water. This line can cut through fins and flippers, immobilize individuals leading to drowning, or become tangled on obstacles in the environment.[5] Young and old dolphins may ingest fishing hooks or lures, causing the animal to be impaled by the hooks or strangled by the attached line or broken terminal tackle. Unnecessarily long float lines attached to crab traps also entangle and drown dolphins.

Boats can be a source of mortality or serious injury for bottlenose dolphins in inshore waters. For example, about 4–5 percent of Sarasota Bay resident dolphins bear scars from boat collisions.[6] These collisions tend to happen around the Fourth of July, when a high-speed boat race occurs that brings thousands of spectator boats into the waters used by the Sarasota resident dolphins and their newborn calves. In recent years, the advent of shallow-draft, high-speed vessels such as personal watercraft and flats boats (small, low recreational fishing boats designed to operate in shallow areas such as sea grass meadows) has increased the risk of collision for dolphins (as well as manatees and sea turtles) using very shallow waters, as there is no opportunity to dive beneath these vessels to avoid them.

Boats pose another threat to dolphins in addition to collision risk. Powerboats can also be a source of disturbance to the animals, leading to disruption of activities, changes in behavior, and possible interference with the animals' use of acoustics. Researcher Stephanie Nowacek reported that dolphins in Sarasota Bay have a powerboat passing within approximately 100 m (about 100 yards) of them once every six minutes during daylight hours, on average. This level of traffic leads to changes in surfacing, respiration, and dive behavior by the dolphins—typically the dolphins stay underwater longer when boats approach. In very shallow waters, dolphins change their heading and swim speed in response to approaching boats. The long-term effects of these repeated responses to disturbance, in terms of impacts to health or reproduction, remain to be determined.[7]

Human interactions with marine mammals can take a variety of forms, as explained in chapter 3. Free-ranging bottlenose dolphins are subjected to illegal harassment or other disruptions by people attempting to feed them or swim with them in several places in Florida. Though these activities may seem innocuous at first consideration, they can lead to changes in the behavior of the dolphins, and can place them at greater risk to other adverse human interactions by attracting them to dangerous situations or causing them to ingest inappropriate and dangerous items that can make them ill or kill them. The situation is analogous to that of feeding bears in parks, where the changes in bear behavior after they begin to be fed often lead to the death or necessitate the removal of the bears. Both feeding and swimming with dolphins in the wild are illegal under the law or against government regulations, and therefore subject to hefty fines.

Coastal development is a threat of unknown magnitude to Florida dolphins. Alteration of shorelines, dredge and fill operations to create waterfront real estate at the expense of sea grass meadows or mangrove fringing forests, and blockage of natural water flows dramatically change the habitat of dolphins and their prey. Because much of Florida's coastal development occurred prior to the advent of field studies of dolphins, there is little quantitative information available on changes in dolphin distributions or abundance relative to habitat change. However, in areas such as Sarasota Bay, dolphin densities are significantly greater in those areas less altered by humans than in the highly developed areas.

Historically, Florida has been the site of extensive commercial collection of bottlenose dolphins for public display in oceanaria, for use in research labs, or for military applications. Well over 1,200 dolphins have been collected from Florida waters since the 1930s,[8] with the most recent collection occurring in 1988. Because of the tendency to select young females, repeated collections from localized areas posed threats to resident communities, leading to a quota system under the Marine Mammal Protection Act limiting collections by gender. Long-term observations of dolphin social structure and reproductive success in Sarasota Bay suggest that removal of certain age or sex classes of dolphins can have significant consequences for the remaining dolphins of the community. Female reproductive success is greater when nursery groups are larger and more stable. Males that are unable to establish a pair-bond with another male may suffer from higher mortality and lower reproductive success than pair-bonded animals. Since 1988, successful captive breeding programs have met the needs of public display and research programs in the United States, alleviating pressure for continued collection from the wild. However, commercial collection continues in other parts of the world, including along mainland coasts and around islands of the Caribbean Sea.

One of the most serious but least-understood threats to bottlenose dolphins is from environmental contamination. Potentially dangerous microorganisms from sewage effluent and vessels are found in parts of the dolphins' range. Chemicals of human origin find their way into the bottlenose dolphins' ecosystem through runoff from agricultural, residential, and industrial sources, and from deposition from the air. Chemicals of concern include heavy metals such as lead and mercury, and organochlorine pollutants including PCBs and pesticides such as DDT and their metabolites. Humans have introduced more than 10,000 chemicals into the environment, but the direct effects of these chemicals on dolphins are largely unknown. Dolphins are known to accumulate high concentrations of organochlorines in their tissues such as blubber. Preliminary studies suggest that high concentrations of PCBs and DDT may be related to reduced immune system function in male bottlenose dolphins in Sarasota Bay. Contaminant residue accumulation may also result in increased calf mortality, through transfer of contaminants from mother to calf, especially via milk. These chemicals bind with lipids (fats), leading female bottlenose dolphins to transfer about 80 percent of their own body burden of organochlorines to their calves through their lipid-rich milk during the early stages of lactation. First-time mothers, who pass along the contaminants they have accumulated over their first eight or so years of life, exhibit a much higher rate of calf loss than do experienced mothers, who transfer contaminants acquired during only a couple of years between lactation cycles. However, conclusive cause-effect relationships between specific chemicals at documented exposure levels with specific health or reproductive effects remain to be demonstrated.

Atlantic Spotted Dolphin (*Stenella frontalis*)

Physical Description: Atlantic spotted dolphins can be identified by their small size relative to most other dolphins and by the speckles distributed over a gray body. Dorsally, these dolphins are dark gray, with a pale "blaze" below the dorsal fin, and gray sides fading to a light gray or white belly. Speckling develops with age in these animals; young spotted dolphins (less than one year old) are devoid of spots and look very similar to young bottlenose dolphins. Speckle patterns develop with lighter spots against a dark background on top (dorsally), and darker spots against a lighter background below (ventrally). Spotting occurs over the entire body, except on the dorsal fin and flukes. Patterns on older animals include fused speckles and mottled patterns.

These dolphins have a tall, falcate dorsal fin in the middle of their back. The rostrum, with a white tip to the upper jaw, is relatively longer than that of bottlenose dolphins, but shorter and sturdier than those of other members of the genus *Stenella* such as spinner, clymene, or pantropical spotted dolphins. As adults, Atlantic spotted dolphins measure about 7–8 feet (2.1–2.4 m) long and weigh about 240 pounds (110 kg).

Atlantic spotted dolphins differ from pantropical spotted dolphins

(*Stenella attenuata*), which may overlap their range slightly, in that adult *S. frontalis* have white bellies, whereas *S. attenuata* have gray bellies. In addition, *S. attenuata* have darker appendages and a light cape on the peduncle. Body form differs somewhat between the two species, with *S. frontalis* appearing more robust, following the form of bottlenose dolphins. In fact, recent genetic findings suggest that Atlantic spotted dolphins may be more closely related to bottlenose dolphins than to the other, more fine-featured members of the genus *Stenella*.

Distribution and Ranging Patterns: Atlantic spotted dolphins inhabit tropical and warm temperate continental shelf and slope waters of the Atlantic Ocean, Gulf of Mexico, and Caribbean Sea. They have been reported from as far north as New England and as far south as southern

Above and facing page: Atlantic spotted dolphins are frequently encountered in Florida's offshore waters. Sometimes spotted dolphins are seen in large groups. Flip Nicklin and Minden Pictures.

Brazil, with a few reports from the central Atlantic and the west coast of Africa. These dolphins are typically found in water depths of approximately 60 to more than 600 feet (approximately 20–200 m), which in most places around Florida means they will be, on average, at least 4 miles (around 6.5 km) from shore. Along the west coast of Florida, spotted dolphins are commonly observed over the broad continental shelf during the winter, and they sometimes come to within about 19 miles (30 km) of shore when current shifts bring more pelagic water masses closer to shore. They are seen infrequently over the shelf during summer. Off the east coast of Florida, where the shelf is narrower, they have been seen within about ½ mile (1 km) of shore.

In some parts of the species' range, these animals have been studied extensively for more than 15 years. Research by Denise Herzing and colleagues has shown that her study population has been resident to the Bahama Banks for the duration of her study, using both the shallow banks and the nearby slope. These scientists have been able to monitor individuals identified from their dorsal fin features as well as speckling patterns on their bodies.

Abundance: Atlantic spotted dolphins are fairly common in the offshore waters of Florida. Estimates of the numbers of these dolphins specifically in Florida waters are lacking, but NOAA Fisheries estimates that there are a minimum of 2,255 dolphins in the Gulf of Mexico, and about 27,785 dolphins in the western North Atlantic.

Social and Other Behavior: Atlantic spotted dolphins tend to be found in larger groups than bottlenose dolphins. Groups of up to 75 individuals have been reported, but on average the animals are found in groups of 20 or fewer. As with bottlenose dolphins, groups are of fluid composition, and tend to be of mixed sex and age. Studies in the Bahamas have found that repeated associations among some individuals are common; mother-calf pairs form strong multiyear bonds, and males form long-lasting alliances. Spotted dolphins reportedly work cooperatively to herd and capture prey fish, and in aggressive encounters with other cetacean species such as bottlenose dolphins.

Food and Feeding: Small fish and squid are the primary prey of Atlantic spotted dolphins, including anchovies, herring, flounder, razor fishes, and small relatives of mojarra and jacks. As mentioned above, they may cooperate to concentrate schools of small fish at the surface in order to facilitate prey capture. These dolphins (as well as some bottlenose dolphins) sometimes engage in an unusual feeding behavior called crater feeding in which they burrow their "faces" into the sand to capture buried prey fish. During bouts of crater feeding the animals scan the bottom with their echolocation. When prey such as a razor fish is located, the animals dig with their rostra into the sandy bottom, pumping their flukes to drive themselves downward. They sometimes burrow to the level of their eyes before withdrawing from the newly created pit with a fish in their mouth and a cloud of sand. Sometimes crater feeding is engaged in by a number of individual dolphins concurrently, and they may be joined by nurse sharks engaging in a very similar pattern of behavior. In addition to searching for prey in the sea floor, the animals may feed very actively near the surface of the water.

Mortality Factors: Atlantic spotted dolphins are subject to natural mortality from shark predation, and from bites by "cookie cutter" sharks. While these dolphins may occasionally suffer from entanglement in fishing gear, this does not appear to be a significant source of mortality in Florida waters.

Pygmy and Dwarf Sperm Whales (*Kogia breviceps* and *Kogia sima*)

Physical Description: These two species are remarkably different from most other cetaceans, making it easy to determine that an animal on a beach is a *Kogia* of one type or the other. However, the two are remarkably similar, to the point where they can be somewhat difficult to distinguish from one another, especially when swimming in the wild. Each has developed adaptations that make it appear rather shark-like. For example, the head is small and squarish, and the small and underslung lower jaw is positioned such that it does not reach the tip of the head, as occurs in most cetaceans. In addition, behind each eye is a crescent-shaped, white line that is called a false gill because it is positioned in the same place and somewhat resembles a fish gill opening. The similarity to sharks may be useful to reduce predation at sea, but there is at least one instance in which a beached pygmy sperm whale was mistaken for a shark and was stabbed to death with a beach umbrella by a man who thought he was protecting his family from a crazed shark.

Behind and below the false gill on each side of the body is a relatively long pectoral flipper. This location is relatively far forward on the body, compared with that of most other cetaceans. The flukes have a concave trailing edge and a moderately deep notch.

In color, the pygmy and dwarf sperm whales are dark gray dorsally (on the back), lighter gray on the sides, and very light on the belly. This coloration pattern in animals is termed "counter shading" and it serves to make the animal difficult to see whether one is looking down on it from above or up at it from below. The flippers and upper side of the flukes are steel gray. The skin is sometimes described as wrinkled.

There are three primary physical differences in these two species. The first involves their size. The pygmy sperm whale is larger, with adults measuring between about 9 and 13 feet (2.7–3.4 m) long and weighing

An orphaned pygmy sperm whale that was held at Mote Marine Laboratory for 21 months. Note the "false gill" behind the eye. Charles A Manire.

between 700 and 900 pounds (318–408 kg). In contrast, the dwarf sperm whale typically measures only about 7–9 feet (2.1–2.7 m) long and weighs only 300–600 pounds (136–272 kg). Newborn pygmy sperm whales are typically only about 4 feet (1.2 m) long, whereas baby dwarf sperm whales do not generally reach this length.

Other differences involve the number and placement of their teeth. Pygmy sperm whales possess 12–16 pairs of thin, sharp, recurved teeth in the lower jaw and generally no teeth in the upper jaw. The teeth in the dwarf sperm whales are similar in shape to those of the pygmy sperm whale, but dwarf sperm whale teeth are shorter and more slender; in addition, the dwarf species generally has only 7–12 pairs in the lower jaw, but has an additional one to three pairs in the upper jaw.

The other distinctive difference between the two species involves the dimensions of the dorsal fin. In the dwarf sperm whale, it is tall (up to 5 percent of the body length) and somewhat falcate (concave or recurved), with a broad base; it is located near the center of the back. The dorsal fin of the pygmy sperm whale is lower, displaced more toward the flukes, and more prominently falcate.

Distribution and Ranging Patterns: Both species are tropical, subtropical, and temperate in their distribution and are found in waters of both the northern and southern hemispheres. Pygmy and dwarf sperm whales are both offshore species that are relatively rarely identified at sea. Analysis of stomach contents suggests that dwarf sperm whales may frequent waters slightly inshore of those occupied by pygmy sperm whales. They do, however, strand relatively frequently in many parts of the world. In the southeastern United States, the pygmy sperm whale is the second most commonly stranded cetacean, behind only the bottlenose dolphin.

Abundance: NOAA Fisheries' minimum population estimates for these two species suggest fewer than 400 individuals exist in the Gulf of

Mexico and along the U.S. Atlantic coast, but these are likely to be underestimates. The animals' tendency toward deep and long dives decreases their availability to observers at the surface, perhaps biasing estimates downward. Since pygmy and dwarf sperm whales are hard to identify at sea, sightings are reported infrequently. When they are reported, species distinctions are rarely made. However, the frequency with which they are found on beaches in many parts of the world suggests that they are not all that rare.

Social and Other Behavior: It is easy to imagine that, for species seen so rarely at sea, little is known about their behavior. This is precisely the case for the pygmy and dwarf sperm whales.

It seems clear that these little whales are excellent divers, which contributes to the infrequency with which they are reported. Observers who have spotted these whales state that they rise slowly to the surface to breathe, produce a relatively inconspicuous blow, and rest quietly at the surface with their bodies hanging down in the water column. Apparently, pygmy sperm whales float higher in the water, with more of their backs exposed, than do the dwarf sperm whales. If startled, either species may defecate, producing a reddish cloud in the water, rather like the ink that a squid produces when it tries to escape from predators. The production of a reddish cloud of feces led some people to refer to these animals as "firecracker whales."

Both pygmy and dwarf sperm whales are relatively slow swimmers and relatively solitary; those few sightings that have taken place at sea involve one to five animals resting at the surface (a behavior termed rafting). Females and calves seem to be the most lasting social group, and they not infrequently strand together on Florida's beaches. Some females are both pregnant and lactating, indicating that these species of whales may breed annually.

Although some scientists have suggested that these whales migrate seasonally, this has not been confirmed.

Food and Feeding: Pygmy and dwarf sperm whales both feed primarily on squid and octopus (collectively called cephalopods). The sharp and recurved teeth seem admirably suited for securing such quick and slippery prey. Fish and crustaceans are also eaten on occasion.

Mortality Factors and Threats: There are no known large predators on pygmy and dwarf sperm whales, although it would not be surprising if they were eaten by large oceanic sharks or by other cetaceans such as killer whales or pygmy killer whales. Small deepwater sharks known as "cookie cutter" sharks often remove small, elliptical bites of tissue from the whales, leaving distinctive scars when healed.

Stranded *Kogia* rarely survive for long, although one pygmy sperm whale calf (named Ami) maintained at Mote Marine Laboratory survived for 21 months. Pathologists have found that many stranded adults in Florida suffer from a condition in which fibrous connective tissue infiltrates the muscle of the heart. This condition is very similar to what humans with beriberi experience. Beriberi is caused by a thiamine deficiency, and interestingly enough, squid (the primary food of pygmy and dwarf sperm whales) is high in thiamine. Some scientists think that, as these deep water whales move inshore or are actively brought inshore by gyres or currents, they may go for periods of time without feeding, thereby leading to the observed disease of the heart muscle. Of course, scientists remain unsure why such whales appear inshore and strand in the first place.

Right Whale (*Eubalaena glacialis*)

Physical Description: Also called the northern right whale, black right whale, and black whale, this species is quite distinctive. Right whales are rotund animals that can reach lengths of about 56 feet (17 m) and weights approaching an astonishing 100 tons (200,000 pounds; 91,000 kg). Females reach larger sizes than the males. Newborn calves may approach 20 feet (6 m) in length.

Besides their bulk, right whales have other features that set them apart from some other species. For example, right whales are, as the name "black whale" suggests, generally very dark in color, with occasional, irregular white patches, especially on the throat and belly. The flippers are

Photograph of a right whale, showing a line in which the animal has become entangled. New England Aquarium.

Mysticetes, like the right whale shown here, possess two blowholes. The toothed whales (odontocetes) have only one. Douglas Nowacek.

quite large and broad, and the flukes have a deep notch between them and a concave rear border. There is no dorsal fin.

The head is enormous, occupying 25 percent or more of the body length. The upper jaw is narrow and strongly arched, the lower jaw is strongly bowed, and the lower lips close over the rostrum (upper jaw) on either side. The baleen is dark and is extremely long—up to nearly 9 feet (2.8 m) long in very large whales—and 220–260 long narrow baleen plates, with long, hairlike grayish fringes on the inside, hang from each side of the upper jaw. As a whale swims with its mouth open at the surface to feed, the baleen may appear pale or white.

The paired blowholes are widely separated. When the whale breathes, the spout is V-shaped, "bushy," and up to about 16.5 feet (5 m) high.

An unusual feature is the presence of prominent wartlike growths called callosities on the head near the chin, near the blowholes, around the eyes, on the lower lips, and on the sides of the head. The most prominent callosities, which lie just in front of the blowholes, are called the bonnet. Parasites called whale lice may occupy the callosities, causing them to appear different colors (white, pink, or orange, for example). Different whales have different callosity patterns, facilitating individual identification by researchers. In addition to the callosities, hairs are numerous on the chin and upper jaw.

Distribution and Ranging Patterns: There are three distinct populations of right whales, found in the North Atlantic Ocean, the North Pacific Ocean, and the southern hemisphere. Obviously, Florida's waters are a seasonal home only to the North Atlantic population.

North Atlantic right whales migrate seasonally. Many individuals spend their summers in waters off New England, Nova Scotia, Newfoundland, Labrador, and possibly southern Greenland. Most of the population occupies feeding habitats in Cape Cod Bay, the Great South Channel and northern edge of Georges Bank east of Cape Cod, the lower

Bay of Fundy, and the Roseway Basin, off southern Nova Scotia. These areas where animals are concentrated represent specially protected critical habitats (a designation allowed under the Endangered Species Act) or conservation areas for right whales.

In winter, pregnant female whales, some other adults, and a few juveniles migrate south to the coastal waters of northeastern Florida and Georgia; there they occupy the only known calving grounds for this population between January and March. Scientists do not know where most of the remaining whales go in winter, although some individuals remain in Cape Cod Bay all winter. On very rare occasions, right whales have been reported from the Gulf of Mexico.

A critical habitat zone has been established to protect right whales in areas where they are most commonly observed in the winter. It extends 15 miles (24 km) offshore from the Altamaha River (just north of Brunswick, Georgia) to just south of Jacksonville, Florida, and then 5 miles (8 km) offshore from that point south to Sebastian Inlet, Florida. Mothers and calves are frequently seen within 5–10 miles (8–16 km) of the coast, and have even been reported within a mile (1.6 km) of the coast in shallow water.

Abundance: The North Atlantic right whale is one of the most endangered whale populations in the world, with fewer than 300 remaining individuals. The population is closely monitored on the feeding grounds in summer and on the winter breeding grounds. Certain individual whales have been monitored for many years.

The name "right whale" was given to these animals because whalers considered them to be the right whales to hunt: they swim slowly, do not dive for long periods of time, float (and were therefore easy for successful whalers to retrieve) when dead, and provide abundant oil, baleen, and other useful products. As a consequence of being optimal quarry for whalers, right whale populations worldwide were severely reduced, primarily during the seventeenth and eighteenth centuries. They have, unfortunately, not really recovered since that time. The two northern populations (Atlantic and Pacific) of right whales total just a few hundred individuals; the southern population, which may originally have numbered 100,000, was also severely decimated but now probably numbers a few thousand animals.

Social and Other Behavior: Most aspects of the social behavior of right whales in the North Atlantic are poorly studied. The bond between a mother and calf is strong and prolonged, lasting several months. The interval between calves averages more than three and a half years and may be as long as five to six years. Thus, although it is possible that right whales live in excess of 100 years, their reproductive potential is low relative to most other species.

Reproductive behavior of right whales is somewhat similar to that of Florida manatees, described above. As many as 40 males energetically attempt to remain close to an estrous female and to mate with her. The males are not aggressive to one another but their level of physical effort and anatomical specializations are impressive. Male right whales possess the largest testes (up to 2,160 pounds [980 kg] in weight for both testes) of any animal in the world. In addition, female right whales may attempt to avoid copulating with males by rolling on their backs, but the extremely long penis (up to 11 feet [more than 3.3 m] long) sometimes allows the males to mate anyway. In this promiscuous mating system, each female may mate with several males when she is in estrus. Mating occurs between August and December.

Historical records suggest that right whales in the North Atlantic formed large groups, numbering 100 or more. With the decimation of the population, groups of two to a dozen are occasionally observed today.

Right whales may be extremely bulky and heavy, but they are also surprisingly acrobatic. They exhibit behaviors such as breaching (leaping clear of the water), flipper-slapping the surface of the water, tail-lobbing (slapping the flukes on the surface or driving them through the surface with great force), and fluke-out dives (dives such that the flukes extend clear of the water). Right whales are not deep or prolonged divers, with maximum submergence times of about 20 minutes. In general right whales swim slowly, not exceeding 12 miles per hour [19.3 kph] even in bursts. Even at such slow speeds, they can cover surprisingly great distances—up to 2,000 miles [3,200 km] in a 43-day period for a radio-tagged female and calf.

Food and Feeding: Right whales, with their long, fine baleen, are specialized feeders. They appear to prefer to eat copepods (small crustaceans that, as a group, are the dominant planktonic herbivores in the sea), but they also consume euphausiids (another group of planktonic crustaceans, including krill, that are abundant in colder waters). Feeding occurs in the summer habitat in the north, rather than in the winter habitat off Florida and Georgia.

Right whales filter-feed at the surface by swimming forward with their mouths open. This behavior is often referred to as "skim-feeding." Because this behavior is expensive energetically, scientists believe that right whales do not feed unless the density of prey exceeds 1,000 organisms per cubic meter (equivalent to about 4 organisms per gallon). Because such densities are not generally found outside the highly productive feeding grounds off New England and Canada, feeding by right whales is not observed off Florida.

Mortality Factors and Threats: Although reports exist of attacks on right whales by killer whales, human activities provide the primary threats to right whales in the North Atlantic.

From 1970 through 2001, 52 dead right whales were reported along the eastern United States and Canada. It has been suggested that the actual number of deaths is probably two to three times that number. Entanglements in fishing gear (primarily in the feeding areas in summer) and collisions with ships cause a significant percentage of the known mortality, even though the numbers of deaths are small—generally one to three animals per year.

However, population models have suggested that the death of a single adult female right whale in a particular year could spell the difference between a stable population and one in decline. A number of federal and state agencies and other organizations are working hard to reduce risks of mortality and serious injury due to entanglement or ship strikes. Unless those efforts are successful, right whales in the North Atlantic may soon disappear forever.

Occasional Visitors to Florida's Coastal Waters

Clymene Dolphin, or Short-snouted Spinner Dolphin
(*Stenella clymene*)

Physical Description: Short-snouted spinner dolphins, also known as clymene dolphins, are among the most recently described cetacean species, having been identified as a species distinct from the spinner dolphin (*Stenella longirostris*) only a little more than two decades ago. Measuring just 6 feet (1.8 m) in length, it is somewhat shorter than the spinner dolphin, but more robust, and has a shorter rostrum and fewer teeth. This species does not seem to be as acrobatic as the aptly named spinner dolphin. Adults weigh about 165 pounds (75 kg) on average. The coloration of this dolphin grades from black dorsally through light gray laterally to white on the belly. A distinctive black band runs from the tip of the rostrum to the melon (forehead), and continues to the blowhole as a lighter gray stripe. Below the black stripe, the beak is gray down to a black border lining the upper and lower jaws, then white ventrally.

Distribution and Ranging Patterns: This species is known from the tropical and subtropical waters of the Gulf of Mexico and Atlantic Ocean. In the latter basin, it has been reported as far south as southern Brazil, as far north as New Jersey, and from the African coast near Senegal. It is found primarily in waters greater than about 800 feet (250 m) deep. Entire groups of clymene dolphins are known to come ashore in events known as mass strandings, but the causes of these occurrences are largely unknown.

Abundance: Because of the difficulties of distinguishing clymene dolphins from spinner dolphins in the wild, estimates of abundance must be viewed with caution. Currently, NOAA Fisheries estimates that 4,120 clymene dolphins inhabit the northern Gulf of Mexico. No estimates exist for the Atlantic Ocean or specifically for Florida waters.

Spinner Dolphin (*Stenella longirostris*)

Physical Description: Spinner dolphins get their name from the characteristic spinning behavior they frequently exhibit. The dolphins leap clear of the water and rotate rapidly around their longitudinal axis, often multiple times before re-entering the water. They exhibit perhaps the greatest geographical variation in coloration and body configuration of any cetacean, leading to the naming of three subspecies. The shape and positioning of the dorsal fin, and the size of a ventral "post-anal keel" (a ridge projecting below the tailstock) are several of the more obvious features that vary from site to site through the species' range. The form found offshore of Florida is similar to that found through much of the world, including the Hawaiian Islands, where they have been studied in great

The aptly named spinner dolphin is among the most acrobatic cetaceans. Randall S. Wells.

detail.[9] Spinner dolphins are small and slender with a very long, thin rostrum, and fairly large and pointed fins. They can reach lengths of more than 7 feet (2.1 m) and weigh more than 200 pounds (90 kg). The coloration of spinner dolphins is very striking, with dark gray to black above, gray along the sides, and white below. A black stripe extends from the eye to the flipper. The upper surface and tip of the rostrum are black, and the underside of the beak is white. All of the fins tend to be dark.

Distribution and Ranging Patterns: The species is found in deep, offshore tropical and warm, subtropical waters around the world, including the Gulf of Mexico and Caribbean Sea, and the Atlantic from New Jersey to Brazil. They typically inhabit waters greater than 330 feet (100 m) deep, but also use the shallow waters of oceanic islands and atolls for resting when these areas are adjacent to deep water. Little is known of the ranging patterns of spinner dolphins off Florida, but around the coast of the Big Island of Hawaii, some individual dolphins have been identified repeatedly over periods of decades.

Abundance: Because of the difficulties of distinguishing spinner dolphins from clymene dolphins in the wild, estimates of abundance must be viewed with caution. Currently, NOAA Fisheries estimates that 4,465 spinner dolphins inhabit the northern Gulf of Mexico. No estimates exist for the Atlantic Ocean or specifically for Florida waters.

Rough-toothed Dolphin (*Steno bredanensis*)

Physical Description: These are dark-colored, intermediate- sized dolphins with a cone-shaped head and prominent beak. They differ from other beaked dolphins in that the head slopes smoothly from the melon to the beak, without the crease that typically delineates the melon from the beak. The name of this dolphin derives from the fine vertical ridges on each tooth, distinguishing them from the smooth teeth of other dolphins. The fins of these dolphins tend to be large; the dorsal fin is located near midbody. A dark back transitions to white on the belly and sides of the face. Light-colored blotches or spots occur on the sides of the animals. Males tend to be larger than females, approaching 9 feet (2.8 m) in length and weighing more than 330 pounds (725 km). In contrast, females may approach 8 feet (2.4 m) in length.

Distribution and Ranging Patterns: Rough-toothed dolphins are found in deep, offshore tropical and warm temperate waters worldwide, including the Gulf of Mexico, the Caribbean Sea, and in the Atlantic Ocean from Virginia to Brazil. Little was known about rough-toothed dolphins in the northeastern Gulf of Mexico until mass strandings occurred in the Florida Panhandle in 1997 and 1998, involving about 10 percent of the estimated Gulf of Mexico population. Satellite-linked radio transmitters tracked stranded dolphins treated at Mote Marine Laboratory in Sarasota and released following rehabilitation back to continental slope waters offshore of the stranding sites. They were tracked through these waters for nearly four months, then were resighted with other dolphins in the same area five months following release, suggesting the existence of a previously undescribed population of rough-toothed dolphins off the northwestern coast of Florida.

Abundance: Rough-toothed dolphins in the northern Gulf of Mexico are estimated to number about 660 individuals. No estimates are available for Florida waters, specifically, or for the western North Atlantic Ocean.

Risso's Dolphin (*Grampus griseus*)

Physical Description: Risso's dolphins are large animals, reaching more than 11.5 feet (3.5 m) in length and approaching 1,100 pounds (500 kg) in weight. They are robust ahead of the dorsal fin, and more slender behind. The flippers are long and pointed, and a tall, narrow, falcate dorsal fin is located in the middle of the back. There is no discernible beak. Among the species' most distinctive features are the vertical V-shaped crease or furrow in the middle of the blunt melon region, and the "battered" appearance of older individuals, as scars and scratches accumulate on the otherwise light gray body. Young Risso's dolphins can be a chocolate brown.

The Risso's dolphin *(top)*, short-finned pilot whale *(middle)*, and false killer whale *(bottom)* look somewhat alike. The grayish-colored bodies of adult Risso's dolphins are often covered with scratches and scars inflicted by other dolphins; the bulbous-headed pilot whale tends to have its dorsal fin well forward and to have a robust, generally black, unscarred body; the false killer has a less bulbous head, a more slender body, and a more caudally placed dorsal fin than the pilot whale. All of these species can exist in very large groups. For more complete diagnostic information see the text. Flip Nicklin and Minden Pictures (pilot and false killer whales) and Randall S. Wells (Risso's dolphin).

Distribution and Ranging Patterns: This dolphin is found worldwide in deep, offshore tropical and temperate waters, including the Gulf of Mexico, Caribbean Sea, and Atlantic Ocean from Newfoundland southward to Argentina. Risso's dolphins are year-round inhabitants of the Gulf of Mexico, especially over the continental shelf, slope, and other waters deeper than about 650 feet (200 m). Little is known of ranging patterns off the Florida coast, but where they have been studied in places such as Monterey Bay, California, some distinctively marked individuals have been identified repeatedly year after year.

Abundance: No estimates of abundance specific to Florida waters are available, but NOAA Fisheries estimates that there are about 22,916 Risso's dolphins in the western North Atlantic and 2,199 in the northern Gulf of Mexico.

Short-finned Pilot Whale (*Globicephala macrorhynchus*)

Physical Description: The short-finned pilot whale is similar in appearance to the long-finned pilot whale, *Globicephala melas,* except that its pectoral flippers are slightly shorter and less bent. It is a large dolphin with a robust body, a bulbous melon, and a large, strongly recurved dorsal fin ahead of the middle of the body. There is no beak. The whales are

uniformly dark (black or gray), except for a light gray anchor-shaped ventral patch under the head, a light "saddle" below and behind the dorsal fin, and a light dorsal chevron behind the head, pointing toward the dorsal fin. Males are significantly larger than females, reaching lengths of greater than 20 feet (about 6 m), whereas females may attain lengths of 18 feet (5.5 m). Males weigh up to 8,000 pounds (3,600 kg); females weigh up to 5,500 pounds (2,500 kg).

Distribution and Ranging Patterns: This species is found in deep, off-shore, tropical, subtropical, and warm temperate waters around the world. It inhabits the Gulf of Mexico (primarily the central and western Gulf), Caribbean Sea, and the Atlantic Ocean from New Jersey southward to Brazil. Short-finned pilot whales tend to be found over the continental slope, in waters about 650 to 3,300 feet (200–1,000 m) deep. Long-finned pilot whales have never been reported from the Gulf of Mexico, and apparently do not venture south of Georgia, so pilot whales seen off Florida are likely all of the short-finned species. Pilot whales are best known from occasional mass strandings in which a few to more than 100 whales beach themselves. The actual causes of mass strandings are still mostly unknown. While such phenomena may involve one or more sick animals, it is believed that the strong social ties may play a role in bringing entire pods ashore along with the sick or injured individuals. Observational and genetic studies of pilot whales in several parts of the species' range have found that some individually distinctive whales can be identified repeatedly in a given area, and female pod membership can be stable over time.

Abundance: Short-finned pilot whales occur in the Gulf of Mexico throughout the year, but in small numbers. NOAA Fisheries estimates that there are about 186 short-finned pilot whales in the northern Gulf of Mexico, and 11,343 in the western Atlantic Ocean. No estimates are available specifically for Florida waters.

False Killer Whale (*Pseudorca crassidens*)

Physical Description: These large dolphins are about the same color and length as, but more slender than short-finned pilot whales. The head is rounded but narrower than that of pilot whales, and protrudes beyond the lower jaw. The tall, falcate dorsal fin is located just behind the center of the body. The flippers have a characteristic broadening at the middle of the leading edge. The whales are mostly black or dark gray except for small amounts of white around the lips and under the head. Males are larger than females, reaching up to about 20 feet (6 m) in length and 5,500 pounds (2,500 kg) in weight. In contrast, females rarely exceed about 16 feet (5 m) in length.

Distribution and Ranging Patterns: This species occurs worldwide in deep, offshore, tropical and temperate waters, including the Gulf of Mexico, the Caribbean Sea, and the Atlantic Ocean from Maryland southward to Argentina. False killer whales are generally found in waters more than about 650 feet (200 m) deep. They occasionally engage in mass strandings in Florida waters.

Abundance: False killer whales are seen infrequently in the northern Gulf of Mexico, where NOAA Fisheries estimates indicate that about 236 whales may occur. No estimates of abundance specifically for Florida waters or the western North Atlantic currently exist.

Pygmy Killer Whale (*Feresa attenuata*)

Physical Description: Though much smaller, pygmy killer whales resemble false killer whales in coloration and shape. These slender black or dark gray dolphins also have a narrow, rounded head, and lack a beak. The head extends slightly beyond the tip of the lower jaw. The dorsal fin,

The pygmy killer whale is rare in Florida's waters. Although it resembles the false killer whale, it may be recognized by its small body and white lips. Flip Nicklin and Minden Pictures.

located near the middle of the back, is tall and falcate, and the pectoral flippers have rounded tips. White pigmentation occurs on the belly, chin, and around the lips. Males are larger than females, reaching lengths of up to 9 feet (2.7 m) and weights of more than 500 pounds (225 kg). Females may attain 8 feet (2.4 m) in length and 440 pounds (200 kg) in weight.

Distribution and Ranging Patterns: Pygmy killer whales are found in deep, offshore tropical waters around the world. They are known from the Gulf of Mexico and in the Atlantic Ocean from the Carolinas southward to Argentina. They are seen most often in waters deeper than about 1,600 feet (500 m).

Abundance: Pygmy killer whales are not numerous in the waters off Florida. NOAA Fisheries estimates that about 285 of these dolphins inhabit the northern Gulf of Mexico. They are seen infrequently in the western North Atlantic Ocean. No estimates exist for the abundance of this species specifically in Florida waters.

Mesoplodont Beaked Whales (*Mesoplodon* spp.)

Physical Description: The beaked whales of the genus *Mesoplodon* are among the least-known marine mammals. They occupy deep, offshore waters and are extremely proficient divers, so people encounter them infrequently. Many species look alike, so distinguishing them at sea can be very difficult. Within the past decade, two completely new species of this genus have been described! Perhaps the main reason we know little about them is that they were never the basis of commercial harvest—and people tend to know a lot about those species or issues that involve the making of money. No specific population estimates exist for any of the species of *Mesoplodon,* but NOAA Fisheries estimates that there are at least 2,419 beaked whales of the combined genera *Mesoplodon* and *Ziphius* in the North Atlantic.

Despite our relative lack of knowledge about these animals, they are beautiful, streamlined, and exquisitely adapted to their deep-diving lifestyle. The genus name refers to the fact that many species possess only a single, flattened tooth in either side of the lower jaw and that the teeth of some species lie along the length of the jaw, not at the tip. In females, the teeth rarely even erupt from the gums, but in the males of some species, the teeth become massive and may even (in the strap-toothed whale) extend upward and curl over the upper jaw, preventing the animal from opening its mouth fully.

The unusual number and dimensions of the teeth raise questions about how mesoplodonts feed. It appears that they feed primarily on squid, and well-developed throat muscles appear to permit at least some species to generate sufficient suction to suck nearby squid into their open mouths without using the teeth at all.

The position, shape, and size of the teeth (where visible) help distinguish among the more than a dozen species of mesoplodonts. Their body size, extent of bodily scarring, and coloration are also distinguishing factors. However, before describing some species differences, we shall note those features that help diagnose a beached specimen as a mesoplodont in the first place.

The first clue, as noted, is the existence of few or no visible teeth; the teeth themselves are sometimes quite unusual. A second very distinctive feature is the presence of two throat grooves (one on either side) that run roughly parallel to the lower jaw bones to form a V. The mesoplodont body is noticeably spindle shaped (fusiform), and the head is small, with a pronounced beak. The large, powerful flukes generally lack a median notch, and they tend to have a rear margin that is straight across or slightly concave. The pectoral flippers are small and fit into depressions called flipper pockets along the side of the animal.

Beaked whales, like this densebeak whale, are uncommonly encountered because they occupy deep waters. Recent strandings of beaked whales have been linked by some to intense sounds produced by human activities. Flip Nicklin and Minden Pictures.

In the early years of the twenty-first century, there have been some strandings that have involved multiple species of beaked whales in a single location. One of these events occurred in March 2000, in the Bahama Islands and involved 17 cetaceans, 14 of them beaked whales. This event and some others (e.g., a stranding in the Canary Islands, September 2002) have occurred coincidentally with military activities in the area and have led to speculation that such activities may actually have caused the whales to strand and die.

The most commonly stranded mesoplodonts on Florida's beaches are as follows:

Blainville's beaked whale (*M. densirostris*): Also called the densebeak whale, this species reaches a length of a little over 15 feet (4.6 m). Males and females reach the same size. In adult males, in particular, the lower jaw becomes strongly arched about halfway along its length, with a single enormous, forward-directed tooth near the point at which the arch begins. The teeth may sometimes have barnacles growing on them. The head, in front of the blowhole, appears more flattened than in most other beaked whales. The body is dark gray or black on the back, with a lighter belly. Light-colored blotches, scratches, and scars may be found over the body; scarring and larger light or reddish patches on the head are more evident in males. This species is widely distributed in temperate and tropical oceans of the world.

Gervais' beaked whale (*M. europaeus*): This species reaches slightly longer body lengths (more than 16 feet; 5 m) than does the densebeak whale. The body of Gervais' beaked whale is dark gray dorsally and lighter on the sides and belly, with a few light markings on the belly, especially around the genital area. Scars may occur, but are not abundant. The tooth of the male may be seen

The protruding teeth of this adult male densebeak whale are encrusted with barnacles. Randall S. Wells.

about one-third of the way from the tip of each side of the lower jaw. The teeth are not large, but they may protrude outside the mouth in adult males. This species is found in temperate and tropical waters of the Atlantic Ocean.

True's beaked whale (*M. mirus*): Relative to the other mesoplodonts found in Florida's waters, True's beaked whale is the largest, reaching a length of up to 18 feet (5.5 m). The teeth of this species are located at the tip of the lower jaw and, not surprisingly, are most apparent in adult males in which the teeth are angled forward and visible outside the mouth. The body is a little more robust than is the case for other mesoplodonts found in Florida. The body coloration is dark gray or black on the back (but perhaps not as dark as in Gervais' and Blainville's beaked whales), a lighter gray on the sides, and lighter still on the belly. The forehead has a slight bulge, a prominent beak, and a small indentation around the blowhole. True's beaked whale appears to occupy temperate waters in the Atlantic and southwestern Indian Oceans.

Sowerby's beaked whale (*M. bidens*): This species reaches lengths of about 16 feet (5 m), and it possesses teeth located about midway along each side of the lower jaw, near the back part of the so-called mandibular symphysis, where the two sides of the lower jaw join. The teeth typically point backward, and then forward; they are large enough to be visible outside of the closed mouth. Neither the coloration nor the external features of the head of Sowerby's beaked whale make it easy to distinguish from some other species, such as Gervais' beaked whale. Light splotches appear on the body.

Goosebeak Whale (*Ziphius cavirostris*)

Physical Description: The goosebeak whale is perhaps the beaked whale most likely to be encountered off Florida. It is larger than the mesoplodonts, with females reaching lengths of up to 24.5 feet (7.5 m) and males being slightly shorter. Similar to the mesoplodonts, the goosebeak whale has the V-shaped throat grooves, a spindle-shaped body, small pectoral flippers, and flukes that lack a well-defined notch and are slightly concave along the trailing edge. Like True's beaked whale, the goosebeak whale has one tooth located at the tip of each side of the lower jaw. However, in goosebeak whales, the teeth are conical, rather than flattened, and the tip of the lower jaw extends beyond that of the upper jaw. Goosebeak whales have a short beak that seems to become less well defined with age. The robust body is often covered with scars that occur during fighting with other goosebeak whales, and from "cookie cutter" sharks. Coloration is somewhat variable, but is often dark brown or slate gray above and a little lighter on the belly. The head of older males may be paler than the rest of the body.

Distribution and Ranging Patterns: The goosebeak whale is one of the most widely distributed species of cetaceans. Due to the relative infrequency with which the species is observed either at sea or stranded on beaches, information regarding migratory or other behaviors is incomplete. Groups of about two dozen animals are sometimes reported at sea, but smaller groups, or solitary animals, seem to be the norm.

Abundance: There are no estimates of abundance for this species, but NOAA Fisheries has estimated a minimum of 2,419 members of the combined genera *Ziphius* and *Mesoplodon* exist in the North Atlantic.

Sperm Whale (*Physeter macrocephalus*)

Physical Description: A sperm whale was the legendary quarry of Captain Ahab in Herman Melville's *Moby Dick*. Indeed, a great deal is known about sperm whales, partly because of the fact that they have been intensively hunted around the globe since the era of Yankee whaling began in the early 1700s. A moratorium on commercial whaling in 1982 put an end to most hunting of sperm whales around the world.

The species is the largest odontocete (toothed whale), and it exhibits extreme sexual dimorphism. Adult males historically reached lengths of 59 feet (18 m) although presently few animals exceed 49 feet (15 m). Females are much smaller, rarely exceeding 39 feet (12 m) in length. Sperm whales are rather bulky, in addition to being long: males may weigh as

The massive and powerful sperm whale, long sought by U.S. and other whalers, was made famous by Herman Melville in *Moby Dick*. Flip Nicklin and Minden Pictures.

much as 43.5 tons (87,000 pounds; almost 39,500 kg) and females, though much smaller, can tip the scales at weights approximating 13.5 tons (27,000 pounds; 12,250 kg). Newborn sperm whales can measure up to nearly 15 feet (4.5 m) long and weigh about a ton (2,000 pounds; 907 kg).

The sperm whale is one of the most distinctive species of cetacean. Its large size provides one clue as to the identity of a sperm whale, but other attributes help as well. The head is enormous, constituting perhaps 25–33 percent of an individual animal's total length (the head in males is proportionally larger than that in females). The species name "macrocephalus" actually means "large head." The lower jaw does not reach the tip of the head, and it contains 18–25 pairs of large, conical teeth that fit into sockets located in the upper jaw. The upper jaw generally lacks teeth.

The single blowhole is located well to the left of the body midline, at the tip of the animal's squared-off head. It produces a rather low, bushy blow that emerges at a sharp angle, pointing toward the left and ahead of the whale.

The body of a sperm whale lacks a dorsal fin, but instead possesses a rounded, or even triangular, "dorsal hump" located about two-thirds of the way back toward the flukes. Behind the hump are a series of "knuckles" or "crenulations." The hump and knuckles are visible as a whale dives; so, at times, are the flukes, which are broad and triangular, with a deep notch between them.

The skin is deeply wrinkled (often described as corrugated), and is dark gray to brown in color. There may be white patches around the mouth or on the belly.

The sperm whale is renowned for many things: its appearance, its importance to whalers, and its adaptations. Among the latter is an uncanny ability to dive to depths of 10,500 feet (about 2 miles; 3,200 m) and for durations exceeding an hour. In addition, recent attention has been given

Except for some males, sperm whales tend to be extremely social animals. Flip Nicklin and Minden Pictures.

to sperm whale social structure, which centers around stable matriarchal groups of females and young. A single large male (called a bull) typically attends each group for short periods of time, and most males occur in bachelor herds, separate from the females and calves. The social system has been likened to that of elephants.

Distribution and Ranging Patterns: Sperm whales are found in virtually all oceans of the world. Only in areas characterized by pack ice are sperm whales absent. Historically, sperm whales were frequently harvested in the Bahamas, and a commercial fishery for sperm whales operated in the Gulf of Mexico during the late 1700s to the early 1900s.

Abundance: There are probably in the neighborhood of a million sperm whales in existence worldwide. NOAA Fisheries estimates a minimum population size of 3,505 in the North Atlantic, and at least 411 sperm whales in the northern Gulf of Mexico. Because of the deep and long-duration dives of this species, population estimates based on observations at the surface may be underestimates. Despite the number of sperm whales that exist, the species is considered to be endangered.

Humpback Whale (*Megaptera novaeangliae*)

Physical Description: The humpback whale is one of the most distinctive species of cetacean, as well as one of the marine mammals with which the general public relates best. The haunting "songs" that male humpbacks produce on the breeding grounds have provided the background for songs (e.g., Judy Collins's "Farewell to Tarwathie"[10]) and have been the basis of entire albums. The acrobatic leaps, which propel humpback whales impressively out of the water, have helped to make humpback whale watching a major industry off the coasts of New England, Hawaii, Alaska, and elsewhere in the United States. It is difficult not to be awestruck when considering the beauty of humpback whales, as well as the unbelievable power it takes to propel a 40-ton (80,000-pound; 36,288 kg) body clear of the water's surface. Less conspicuously, humpback whales commonly lie at the surface with their long pectoral flippers extending out of the water, occasionally slapping their flippers or flukes loudly on the surface.

As is the case for most mysticetes, female humpback whales may reach somewhat greater body lengths (about 52.5 feet [16 m]) than males (almost 49 feet [15 m]). The reason for this presumably has to do with the greater energy demands on females due to gestation and lactation and the fact that a larger animal has both a lower weight-specific metabolism[11] and a greater energy storage capacity than a smaller one. As is the case with right whales and other mysticetes, humpback whales feed heavily for just a few months each year in areas where food resources are densely concentrated. During the remaining months, the animals fast or feed very sparingly. With newborn calves measuring a robust 16 feet (5 m) long and weighing a couple tons (4,000 pounds; 1,800 kg), the energetic demands on female whales due to either gestation or lactation are hardly imaginable. After nearly a year of suckling, the calf is weaned at almost twice its neonatal length.

In addition to large size and very acrobatic behavior, some features that set humpbacks apart from many other species include the following: the presence of extremely long flippers, measuring about one-third the total body length and typically white or mostly white, with knobs along the leading edge; the presence of 14 to 35 broad grooves on the underside of the body, which extend from the tip of the lower jaw to the area of the navel; the existence of a prominent bump near the tip of the lower jaw; a robust, generally dark-colored body, with some white areas on the throat and belly; the presence of 270–400 baleen plates, which can measure a little over 2 feet (up to 70 cm) long and are generally black, with black or olive-black bristles; the flattened nature of the head in front of the blowhole; the existence of knobs atop the head; a blow that is low (less than 10 feet [3 m] high) and "bushy"; the fact that the flippers and flukes are scalloped along the trailing edge; the presence of a small dorsal fin, which varies in shape among individuals; and the fact that humpbacks commonly raise their flukes clear of the water when they dive.

The latter feature has provided an important basis for studies of humpback whales. On the underside of the flukes are individually dis-

The humpback whale is well known from documentaries and for its haunting "songs." Humpbacks are very recognizable by their large "winglike" pectoral (front) flippers. Flip Nicklin and Minden Pictures.

The underside of the flukes of humpback whales have distinctive patterns that allow scientists to identify individual animals. To identify individual bottlenose dolphins, scientists use nicks and notches in the dorsal fins, and for manatees scientists use scar patterns on the fluke and body. Randall S. Wells.

tinctive black-and-white patterns. By taking photographs of the under-side of the flukes of diving whales, scientists have been able to develop comprehensive catalogs of the individual whales that make up particular humpback populations around the world. The catalogs, in turn, provide the data to allow calculations of population sizes, to assess reproductive performance of females, and to better understand migrations, social behavior, and other aspects of humpback biology.

The aerial displays of humpbacks have been noted. In terms of their swimming prowess, these whales are relatively slow (traveling at about 3.5–7.5 miles per hour [6–12 kph]) and cannot dive for more than about 20 minutes, with much shorter-duration dives being the norm.

Distribution and Ranging Patterns: Humpback whales are widely distributed around the world. In the western North Atlantic Ocean, humpbacks are found in the winter months around the West Indies, where they calve and breed. Areas where humpback whales are especially common at this time of year include Silver Bank.

During the summer, the North Atlantic whales occupy the highly productive waters off the coasts of places such as New England, Canada, Greenland, and Iceland. Here, the whales feed on krill and small species of schooling fish (e.g., sand lance).

Off the east coast of Florida, humpbacks are typically found in spring or fall, as they migrate to either the feeding or breeding grounds. Such migrations generally take place over relatively shallow water.

Abundance: Commercial whaling decimated the humpback whale populations of the world. There were probably well over 100,000 humpback whales before the advent of modern whaling; today there are fewer than 10,000, although many populations appear to be growing. In the North Atlantic Ocean, there are more than 2,000 humpback whales, with the majority being found in several stocks on the western side of the ocean. NOAA Fisheries provides a minimum population estimate of 568 humpback whales in the Gulf of Maine stock, the one that spends most of its time in waters under U.S. jurisdiction.

Humpback whales are considered to be endangered. They typically produce a calf every other year or so, although some individuals appear to have produced a calf in successive years. This represents a faster reproductive rate than is the case for many cetaceans.

Causes of death among humpback whales appear to be relatively few in number. Killer whales are the only natural predators of adults that have been documented. Human-related mortality is more common, and is due to entanglement in fishing gear, collisions with ships, and even subsistence hunting in some parts of the world.

Pinnipeds

There are no pinnipeds that are considered natural residents of Florida. There are three main groups (families) of pinnipeds: otariids, phocids, and odobenids.

The otariids include the sea lions and fur seals, characterized by several features: external ears, dense fur, the ability to rotate their hind flippers under them and move about well on land; and large front flippers. The phocids are sometimes called the true seals or earless seals. Phocids lack an external ear flap, have relatively sparse fur, possess a very streamlined (spindle-shaped) body, with small front flippers, and cannot position their hind flippers to be able to walk on all four limbs on land. The odobenids include just one species, the highly distinctive walrus.

In Florida, people in the mid-1900s reported an occasional feral California sea lion (an otariid; *Zalophus californianus*) that had escaped from a public display facility. No recent sightings of sea lions have occurred in Florida to the best of our knowledge. In recent years, however, sightings of phocid pups (mostly of hooded seals, *Cystophora cristata*, but also including some harbor seals, *Phoca vitulina*) have become more common. There are two reasons occasionally given for the increase in hooded seal sightings: (a) cool water temperatures in some recent winters have been conducive to hooded seals appearing farther south than usual; and (b) more likely, population growth in recent years of several phocid species including hooded seals, harbor seals, harp seals (*Phoca groenlandica*) and gray seals (*Halichoerus grypus*) in New England and eastern Canada may have precipitated some range expansion.

Rarities in Florida's Waters

Several species appear on very rare occasions in the coastal waters of Florida or on Florida's beaches. They include three mysticetes (Bryde's whale, *Balaenoptera edeni;* the minke whale, *Balaenoptera acutorostrata;* and the fin whale, *Balaenoptera physalus*) and several odontocetes (the killer whale, *Orcinus orca;* the striped dolphin, *Stenella coeruleoalba;* Fraser's dolphin, *Lagenodelphis hosei;* the melon-headed whale, *Peponocephala electra;* the pantropical spotted dolphin, *Stenella attenuata;* and the harbor porpoise, *Phocoena phocoena*). Because sightings or strandings of these species represent extremely unusual occurrences, we simply list the species, without any description. Interested readers should see Leatherwood and Reeves' *Sierra Club Handbook* or the Reeves et al. *National Audubon Society Guide,* which we noted earlier, for descriptions of these species.

chapter 3

Threats and Protection

IN AUGUST 2003, the U.S. Marine Mammal Commission held an unprecedented event: a consultation to look proactively at issues likely to jeopardize the health and well-being of marine mammals decades from now, and to recommend to the U.S. Congress and appropriate agencies creative, forward-looking approaches to research that will provide decision makers with reliable information for management and conservation. The Marine Mammal Commission, the federal agency with oversight for all marine mammal activities in the United States, hopes that this event will help decision makers to avoid the crisis-oriented approach that currently characterizes so much natural resource management.

To put matters into context, let's step back only about 30 years, to 1972 and the passage of the Marine Mammal Protection Act (MMPA). The MMPA was itself an unprecedented piece of legislation, since it was the first U.S. law to take an ecosystems perspective to managing and conserving living marine resources, rather than focusing on one species at a time, independent of its ecosystem. A fundamental approach to effective management of marine mammals under the act involves maintaining healthy marine ecosystems. A stated goal of the MMPA is that no population of marine mammals be allowed to diminish beyond the point at which it ceases to be a significant functioning element of the ecosystem it occupies. The law further states that marine mammal populations should be maintained within their optimum sustainable population level, defined as a range of population sizes between the carrying capacity of the environment and the population at which net reproduction is highest. The authors of the MMPA had lofty, visionary, and admirable goals that unfortunately were difficult to reach given the state of knowledge about marine mammals at that time.

Imperfect knowledge about marine mammals in 1972 was paralleled by incomplete perceptions about threats to marine mammals at that time. In fact, the MMPA was catalyzed by public and scientific concern about the effects of three primary human activities: commercial whaling (which the United States ceased doing only in 1971),[1] clubbing of baby harp seals, and the killing of hundreds of thousands of dolphins each year by yellowfin tuna fishermen.

Thirty years later, knowledge is better, but still imperfect; however, to the planners of the 2003 workshop, it was abundantly clear that myriad threats exist for marine mammals. Nearly a dozen categories of threats formed the basis of discussions at the workshop. Among the more serious issues were the following: (1) the effects of more and more anthropogenic (produced by humans) noise being directed into marine and estuarine systems; (2) competition for resources between humans and marine mammals; (3) killing or serious injury of marine mammals as a result of human activities such as fishing and boating; (4) the amounts and types of chemical toxicants people introduce into aquatic systems; (5) the increasing occurrence of harmful algal blooms such as red tides; (6) disease and parasitism; (7) dramatic habitat alteration, as occurs during coastal development, or dredge and fill; (8) global climate change; and (9) the inevitable and sometimes subtle changes that occur simply as a consequence of having more and more people occupying the earth. Whereas the commercial harvest of marine mammals constituted the greatest perceived threat to most species of marine mammals just a few decades ago, the range of threats today is just a little staggering to consider.

What makes the whole situation even more difficult is the fact that some complex interactions among the issues may make their impacts even worse than imagined. For example, harmful algal blooms and dead zones (waters where oxygen levels are extremely low or nonexistent, resulting in little life in those areas) have probably occurred at least to some extent throughout much of earth's history. Today, however, pollution— primarily agricultural runoff—may exacerbate the frequency or intensity with which such events occur. The increase in runoff itself relates both to human population increases and to technological "advances" in fertilizers and other chemicals we use to better support the agricultural needs of our population. On the other hand, red tides and dead zones may kill many organisms, including some of commercial importance, and may concentrate the distribution of others; the latter, of course, can affect distribution of fishing effort and lead to regional problems for marine mammals associated with incidental take in nets or with competition for food. In our increasingly complex world, the problems can become incredibly difficult to diagnose, study, and mitigate. Many seem to be of such magnitude and difficulty that a concerned individual might well wonder: what can I do to minimize the harm?

In Florida's coastal and inland waters, all of the threats identified by the workshop exist to one degree or another (see "Mortality Factors and Threats" for species such as bottlenose dolphins and manatees in chapter 2). The presence of high levels of mercury and other pollutants in some parts of the state is extremely worrisome, and red tides have killed as many as 150 manatees (not to mention numerous dolphins, turtles, fish, and birds) in a single year. Commercial and recreational fishing leads to entanglement and death or injury of Florida's marine mammals, and the effects of competition for food on the animals are unknown, but quite possible. One has only to glance at the extent to which Florida's coastline and intracoastal waterways are seawall lined and dissected into orderly canals to perceive something of the extent to which a productive shore lined with mangroves has been altered to accommodate 16 million human residents. And the presence of roughly a million registered boats and tourist boats contributes to significant levels of noise, disturbance, injury, and mortality of manatees, right whales, bottlenose dolphins, sea turtles, and even other humans.

The threats to humans themselves often become obscured in the news. The threats to marine mammals—chemical pollution; noise/disturbance; toxic algal blooms; reductions in primary productivity and subsequent reductions in availability of food; habitat alteration; boating accidents—all threaten people as well. For example, there has been an incredible amount of attention paid to the extent to which watercraft collisions kill and seriously injure a variety of marine mammals, especially manatees, in Florida. Little is ever written or said about the fact that Florida generally leads the country in the number of human fatalities associated with watercraft accidents—a sad statistic that becomes even worse when it is recognized that the number of boats registered in Florida isn't even the highest in the country.[2] This one example simply serves to illustrate that most things that threaten the health and well-being of marine mammals around the world ultimately threaten our own species' health and well-being too.

Finally, the extent to which tens to hundreds of thousands of well-intended people try to interact with free-ranging marine mammals by swimming with, feeding, or touching the animals is having some subtle as well as overt effects. This problem also exists elsewhere, but in Florida, exposing marine mammals directly to the public has become big business and accepted practice. In chapter 4 we discuss what we consider to be more benign approaches.

One other topic may bear mentioning. Scientists who work with marine mammals are sometimes permitted (as authorized by the Marine Mammal Protection Act or the Endangered Species Act, discussed below) to conduct activities that involve close approaches to marine mammals and even the brief capture of animals for tagging or health assessments, followed by release. The regulatory agencies with responsibility for these animals must judge that the research being conducted carries sufficient benefits that it merits the cost in terms of disruption of the animals. In addition, the regulatory agencies are careful to ensure that the cumulative work of various scientists does not unduly affect the animals being studied. The scientists who are permitted to work with marine mammals are accountable, through regular reports to the agencies, for their actions.

The State of the "Natural" World

In 1998, people around the United States celebrated the Year of the Ocean. Our love for our seas, bays, and estuaries certainly merited some celebration. Millions of people rely on our waterways for their livelihoods, as aesthetic resources, or simply as a place to unwind. The federal government, in fact, compiled considerable information about our seas and coastlines, noting some impressive statistics.[3]

For example, about half of the United States population lives and works in coastal areas, a figure that will rise to 75 percent by the year 2025. In addition, 180 million people visit our nation's coastlines annually, and travel and tourism currently represent the largest and fastest-growing part of the service industry in the country. One in six jobs in the United States is marine related.

Thus, our coastal areas receive frequent, if not always good, use by people. Future projections get a little scary, though, to those of us who would like our coastlines to continue to be good places to live, visit, and work. The federal report continues by noting that many coastal areas will become "sprawling, interconnected metropolitan centers." In U.S. waters, and indeed around the world, many fisheries are already at or over their capacity, and the effects of commercial fishing have had enormous but poorly recognized ecological impacts.[4] Bacterial contamination caused

2,500 closings and advisories for coastal bathing beaches in the United States during 1996. And the report ominously notes that the government simply cannot do all that needs to be done to mitigate damages and prevent problems of the future.

Does this mean that the natural world is doomed? Not necessarily. Equally gloomy figures could have been offered for some developed areas of Florida in the past. In Tampa Bay, for example, most of the sea grasses disappeared and poor water quality made it impossible to see the bottom in many locations in the 1970s. Cleanup programs reversed the dismal trend and allowed the amount and quality of resources to improve.

The point is that people can decide to make a difference in the quality of their environment. Changes in human attitudes toward resources and in human motivation to strike a better balance between human activities and conservation will be keys to future enjoyment of natural resources by Floridians and others in the United States and around the globe.

In mid-2002, several prominent scientists were asked for their views on the earth's state of health. Their responses highlighted causes for both optimism and despair. Ultimately, the salvation of the planet in the face of increasing pressures brought by our burgeoning population lies in phrases used by the scientists: "change our ways"; "awaken the public"; "concentrate peoples' minds"; and make a "commitment to restoring environmental stability and peace to the world."[5] Clearly the state of the world is related to the state of our collective minds . . .

The Rules and Regulations: Legislation and Agency Responsibilities

There are several laws that relate to Florida's marine mammals and their environment in one way or another. The three that are most frequently invoked are two federal laws (the Marine Mammal Protection Act and the Endangered Species Act) and the Florida Manatee Sanctuary Act.

The Marine Mammal Protection Act has already been mentioned. It is the most comprehensive law protecting marine mammals in the United States. The MMPA is noteworthy, as mentioned, for its ecosystem perspective and for suggesting that marine mammals be maintained at their optimum sustainable population level. In addition, the MMPA is distinctive because, perhaps more than any other federal environmental law, it mandates involvement of science and scientific experts to facilitate effective decision making.[6]

Another distinctive, but extremely useful, premise of the MMPA is that the so-called burden of proof in wildlife management and conservation is, or should be, on the user.[7] Effectively this means it is clear that there are certain individuals or groups who benefit financially from most human activities that affect wildlife or habitat. Rather than expecting the general public or agencies (using taxpayer revenues) to show conclusively that those activities do jeopardize marine resources or habitat, the MMPA and some other laws suggest that the burden should be on potential beneficiaries to demonstrate that their activities do not unduly affect the resources in question. Implemented well, the burden of proof approach can be a powerful tool both to save taxpayer money and to promote effective conservation; sadly it is rarely implemented. It is a topic that is explored somewhat more fully in a number of references, including *Mysterious Manatees*.

The MMPA fundamentally approaches protection of marine mammals by prohibiting their taking, defined to include harassment, hunting, capturing, killing, or attempting to harass, hunt, capture, or kill. To be sure, there are provisions that provide exemptions; for example, as noted above, scientists can apply for permits that allow them to conduct such activities as capturing and releasing marine mammals to assess their body condition or to attach tags and transmitters; commercial fishermen occasionally capture and even kill marine mammals during netting operations; and Alaska Natives and members of the Makah tribe in Washington are permitted to hunt and kill marine mammals for subsistence purposes.

The meanings of the words hunt, capture, and kill seem to be pretty clear. The term harassment, however, has led to considerable confusion. The term has generally been taken by managers and scientists to indicate an activity that causes a change in the "normal" behavior of a marine mammal or mammals. As a result of a court case in Texas[8] the feeding of free-ranging marine mammals was explicitly forbidden as a type of harassment (i.e., as a "take"). In addition, NOAA Fisheries has interpreted harassment to include the deliberate steering of watercraft to intercept marine mammals in the water; in other words, if a dolphin or other marine mammal approaches a moving boat, that is fine in the eyes of the law, but for the boat to deviate from its path deliberately to intercept the dolphin constitutes a take.

Many other human activities may also be eliciting harmful responses in marine mammals, however, and therefore constitute a type of harassment as well. Unfortunately, the vagueness of the definition of harassment has led to poor enforcement and general confusion among the public about what is and is not allowed. In the next chapter, we provide some insights regarding activities by people that may inadvertently cause harm to marine mammals, as well as alternatives to such activities.

The MMPA identified those agencies that would carry responsibility for marine mammals in the United States. The Act even created a new agency, the U.S. Marine Mammal Commission, as an independent oversight agency for all marine mammal research and conservation in the country. The commission has a permanent staff of about a dozen people near Washington, D.C., supplemented by three presidentially appointed commissioners and nine scientific advisors.

The Marine Mammal Commission is, as noted, an oversight agency. Other agencies are responsible for conducting or promoting the necessary research to inform wise decision making, as well as for management of marine mammals and enforcement of the MMPA and other laws. NOAA Fisheries (also known as the National Marine Fisheries Service), which is part of the Department of Commerce, is responsible for all cetaceans, as well as for true seals, fur seals, and sea lions. Thus, NOAA Fisheries carries most of the responsibility for marine mammal research, management, and enforcement. The U.S. Fish and Wildlife Service (part of the Department of the Interior), together with the U.S. Geological Survey (also part of Interior), is responsible for research, management, and enforcement associated with the other marine mammals under United States jurisdiction, namely manatees, dugongs, polar bears, sea otters, and walrus. Interestingly enough, a completely different agency carries the primary responsibility for the care and maintenance of captive marine mammals; that agency is the Animal and Plant Health Inspection Service, which recently became part of the Department of Homeland Security.

With so many agencies, one might wonder whether things get confusing at times. The answer is yes! For example, the different agencies interpret and enforce the MMPA and other laws somewhat differently. Perhaps the best example of this involves swimming with dolphins and other marine mammals.

It is clear that, for a hefty price, people can legally swim or wade with bottlenose dolphins at a number of public display facilities in Florida and elsewhere in the United States. Although there are constraints on such activities for the good of both the dolphins and the humans who are involved, swim-with-the-dolphin programs are fully approved by the Animal and Plant Health Inspection Service.[9] So, incidentally, are activities such as the feeding of captive dolphins by the general public.

But when the public encounters a free-ranging dolphin in Tampa Bay or the Indian River Lagoon, do the same rules apply? Certainly, the public cannot legally feed such animals; that explicitly violates the MMPA. However, swimming with free-ranging dolphins is not explicitly forbidden under the act, even though some people have argued that it could constitute harassment (and therefore is categorically illegal). Recently, NOAA Fisheries promulgated rules that interpret the MMPA in this way, so it is likely that enforcement officers may soon start to cite people for swimming with dolphins in the wild. Thus the public needs to understand that what is allowable and legal with captive dolphins is punishable by fines and arrest when done with dolphins in the wild. It would be useful for members of the public to recognize, for their own safety, that there are real differences between interacting with trained animals in a controlled setting and interacting with the same species in the wild, with no controls.[10]

But the confusion doesn't end there. Some officials with the U.S. Fish and Wildlife Service have opined that it *is* permissible to swim with manatees in the wild.[11] In fact, these officials sometimes encourage it as a way for the public to appreciate, and presumably conserve the animals better. So the public is presented with a complex set of dos and don'ts: swimming with and feeding dolphins in captivity is fine; swimming with and feeding manatees in captivity is not; swimming with and feeding dolphins in the wild is illegal; feeding manatees in the wild is illegal, but swimming with them is fine!

The Marine Mammal Commission, in its oversight role, has repeatedly asked the agencies to develop consistent interpretations of the Marine Mammal Protection Act, to enforce the provisions of the Act consistently, and to educate the public about what is and is not permitted, and why. Clearly, a lot still needs to be done!

Before leaving the subject of agency responsibilities and confusion, we make one additional point. NOAA Fisheries is an agency whose primary responsibilities involve fisheries management. The Office of Protected Resources, which works with marine mammals, sea turtles, and a few other species, is just a small part of the agency, and the goals of the office (i.e., protection of particular species) are often in conflict with those of the agency (i.e., promotion of fisheries). Thus, it is often difficult for marine mammal research and protection to have the priority many people wish they did. Similarly, the U.S. Fish and Wildlife Service (FWS) falls under Department of the Interior along with agencies such as the Minerals Management Service, whose goals and directives (e.g., promoting oil and gas development) differ greatly from those of FWS. The point is that it is sometimes difficult, even for very dedicated people, to accomplish all that laws such as the MMPA mandate when the goals and directives of the responsible agencies go against those of "sister" agencies with more money, larger constituencies, and greater power.

The Endangered Species Act (ESA) is the second federal law that is applicable to marine mammals of Florida. Like the MMPA, the ESA can level stiff fines for offenders: up to a year in prison and fines of up to $20,000. Also like the MMPA, the ESA prohibits taking of particular species, and its definition of take is pretty similar to that of the MMPA. However, there are a couple of important differences in the laws, as well.

To begin, the ESA only considers those species or populations that are considered endangered or threatened with extinction. Relatively few of Florida's marine mammals (manatee, right whale, sperm whale, humpback whale) fall under these categories (see the species descriptions in chapter 2). So the ESA is not relevant at this time for most species of marine mammal that the public encounters in Florida, whereas the MMPA applies to and protects them all.

A second key difference is in the definition of "take." The ESA adds a crucial term, "harming," to the list of prohibited types of taking, and then considers the destruction or modification of "critical habitat" as a way in which a listed species or population could be harmed. This means that the ESA provides a very direct way by which certain types of developments, for example, could be blocked, making the ESA an especially unpopular law among certain user groups. This unpopularity has contributed to the fact that the U.S. Congress in more than a decade has not officially reauthorized the ESA.

Another issue central to the ESA is whether, as a species or population is considered for either listing or delisting, the current and future threats to that group have been adequately identified and are under control. If they are considered not to be, then it argues well for keeping a species or population for which numbers are low on the list.

In Florida's coastal waters, for example, it is difficult to argue that threats to habitat or to manatees are under control, when projections by some demographers suggest that the numbers of humans there may double by 2030. Without unprecedented levels of planning, cooperation, and even creativity, that doubling will dramatically affect such things as availability of fresh water, density and distribution of sea grasses, pollution and other aspects of water quality, boat traffic, and stocks of commercially and recreationally important fish and shellfish.

The mandate to look ahead to the future is vital. In today's litigation-oriented society, NOAA Fisheries and the U.S. Fish and Wildlife Service often are forced to respond to the latest crisis-induced lawsuit. When a crisis emerges, it is typical that options are few in number and expensive. Human and other resources become devoted to addressing that crisis and litigation, while other issues are placed on the back burner. Only when the agencies and other groups become able to focus more on the future, to creatively address the issues of the future by developing precrisis databases and cost-effective solutions, will the natural resources issues of the United States and the world really stand a chance of being solved well. Planning well into the future, with the benefit of appropriate data, is essential if we wish to balance the maintenance of human lifestyles and activities with the existence of the natural resources that help contribute to human quality of life.

There are several other federal acts about which readers may want to become more knowledgeable; perhaps key among them is the National Environmental Policy Act. A chapter titled "The laws governing marine mammal conservation in the United States" by Baur, Bean, and Gosliner (see bibliography) provides an excellent overview, but it would be inappropriate for our little volume to provide such details. Two final pieces of legislation about which Floridians and visitors to Florida should be aware, however, are state laws.

Manatees have actually been legally protected in Florida since 1893, around the time when people started to comment on the increasing rarity (due, in large part, to hunting) of the species. The most recent and far reaching of the state laws to protect manatees is the Manatee Sanctuary Act, passed in 1978. This law considers the entire state to be a manatee sanctuary. In order to protect manatees well, the law authorizes managers to go so far as to exclude human activities in particular locations. More generally, the Manatee Sanctuary Act has served as the authority under which boat speeds may become regulated in certain locations where manatees are abundant or where manatee deaths due to boats are frequent. Thus, as people boat in certain waterways around the state, they encounter boat speed zones that have been put into place under the authority of the Florida Manatee Sanctuary Act in an effort to reduce the extent to which manatees are seriously injured or killed by collisions with watercraft.

Obviously, closures and restrictions are controversial, and the state's managers have attempted to do several things: (1) take into account the best available scientific data to justify restrictions; (2) consider the needs and desires of people who live in areas where restrictions are being considered; and (3) focus on the locations (the 13 "key counties") where, based on perceptions when the law was passed in 1978, restrictions are likely to have the greatest impact in terms of manatee protection. The lead agency for implementing and enforcing provisions of the Florida Manatee Sanctuary Act, as well as for conducting research on the species, is the Florida Fish and Wildlife Conservation Commission.

Another state law that is extremely relevant is the Local Government Comprehensive Planning and Land Regulation Act of 1985 (commonly, and informally, called the Growth Management Act). This law requires all coastal counties to develop and implement comprehensive plans that attempt to reconcile the inevitable human population growth in Florida and the protection of natural resources, including manatees. Although the intent of this act was commendable and future oriented, many counties have failed to produce plans, and those county plans that have been prepared and approved to date are sometimes inadequate and superficial. As an unfortunate result of not developing really comprehensive plans (or plans at all) many counties have lost the opportunity for careful, measured assessment and planning, and they may soon be faced with crisis-driven reactions that will create considerable frustration.

Laws and agencies provide a formal structure that attempts to facilitate certain outcomes. It should be clear that not all laws are consistent with one another because they are developed by different people to achieve different goals. It should also be clear that the mandates of many laws are not achieved. People should recognize, though, that changes can come about simply because people want changes. There are plenty of examples in which dedicated people have caused important things to happen that benefit everyone.[12] Trite as it may sound, individuals can make a difference! In our next chapter, we discuss how people can change their behaviors to minimize impacts to marine mammals.

chapter 4

Guidelines for Human Interactions with Florida's Marine Mammals

SHARING THE WORLD of Florida's marine mammals can be accomplished responsibly and yet enjoyably and productively by observance of three simple tenets: (1) remember that we are visitors to the animals' homes, (2) become knowledgeable about and follow established regulations protecting the animals, and (3) use common sense. The suggestions that follow are the opinions of the authors, anchored in current regulations, but informed and shaped by the authors' combined 60-plus years of experience with marine mammal research and conservation. This experience covers the formative years of the field of marine mammal science, and has seen attitudinal changes in the United States that have led to protection of these creatures rather than exploitation through hunting. During this time we have witnessed the near demise of some populations of marine mammals. Entire species of marine mammals, including the baiji, the endemic dolphin of the Yangtze River, and the vaquita, the endemic Gulf of California harbor porpoise, are likely to become extinct within the next few decades, largely as a result of human interactions. Our primary purpose in this chapter is to provide guidance that will help people to use the waters of Florida for their own purposes while at the same time minimizing their impacts on the marine mammals using the same waters. However, we also recognize that people frequently encounter marine mammals that have stranded on Florida's beaches; at the end of the chapter we provide some guidelines for responding to that circumstance.

Implicit in the title of the book is the understanding that both humans and marine mammals will continue to use Florida waters, and that this coexistence can be optimized for all parties. As marine scientists based in Sarasota, Florida, our work requires that we and our staff and students spend thousands of hours each year operating powerboats in Florida waters. This is one of the perks of the job—it is far more enjoyable than the time we spend in meetings or in front of computer monitors. We fully understand and appreciate the sense of freedom that accompanies leaving the dock and heading into the waterways or open waters along Florida's coasts. We do not enjoy some of the constraints that have been placed on this freedom in recent years, such as seemingly interminable slow speed zones, but we have come to appreciate the need for compromise if marine mammals and humans are going to continue to coexist in these waters.

~

Fossil, recent skeletal, and genetic evidence indicates that marine mammals existed in Florida waters for millennia before the current large-scale incursion of humans. Human interactions with marine mammals in Florida waters have occurred only over centuries. Coastal middens provide evidence of at least occasional hunting and consumption of manatees and other marine mammals by the early Native American residents of Florida. The "scrag whale," the Atlantic form of the gray whale, is known from museum specimens from the Atlantic seaboard, including the coast of southeastern Florida. It has been suggested that this whale became extinct in the Atlantic from overhunting about 300–400 years ago.

Interactions have increased exponentially within the last century as humans have come to Florida in ever-increasing numbers as both new residents and vacationers. Coastal development and rapidly increasing numbers of vessels are bringing people into contact with the long-term marine mammal and other natural residents of coastal waters. Shipping, military activities, and industrial development are affecting offshore populations. The implications associated with the fact that humans can come and go from Florida's waters at their choosing, and can change these waters through their actions, whereas the marine mammals require these same waters to survive, are not trivial. Optional human activities for recreation, aesthetic enjoyment, and economic gain take advantage of the waters that are the obligatory home to such creatures as manatees and bottlenose dolphins. Two questions, one practical, the other ethical, must be addressed as the habitats of these animals are changed by human activities. First, are the animals biologically capable of adapting to the recent changes effected by humans? Second, is it appropriate for the burden of changing their way of life to be placed on these animals rather than on the humans, the newest creatures on the scene and the agents of dramatic environmental change? Our suggestion on both points is to use the precautionary principle of respect for the animals' homes, recognizing that we can leave while they likely will not or cannot without serious adverse impacts. How would we expect visitors to our own homes to behave?

This point that humans can choose how they will use marine resources while resident marine mammals are obligated to what is there was recently illustrated to us by a colleague from Texas. He stated that in the area around Galveston Bay, people have been advised to avoid eating locally caught seafood more than a couple of times a week to avoid possible consequences of high levels of water-borne pollutants. Of course, the dolphins that live in the bay must subsist on that same, polluted source of food that poses a danger to people.

The second tenet, that of becoming familiar with and following established regulations protecting marine mammals, can be accomplished in a variety of ways. As discussed in chapter 3, federal and state agencies and local governments have put regulations forward to provide protection for marine mammals. In some cases the public is made aware of regulations through posted signs on the waterways or at shore-side access points. For example, regulatory agencies such as NOAA Fisheries provide guidelines[1] on their Web sites (see below), or through brochures, town hall meetings, and public service announcements. Compliance with the regulations and guidelines remains largely unenforced, given the unfortunate fact that regulatory agency law enforcement divisions are typically understaffed relative to the extent of the coastline and the magnitude of their responsibilities with marine mammals and a variety of other protected and endangered species.

In the absence of adequate public awareness of guidelines and enforcement of regulations, the third tenet, common sense, takes on increasing importance. When considering an interaction with a marine mammal, one should consider whether that interaction is in the best interest of the animal. The safety and well-being of the manatee, whale, or dolphin should at all times take precedence over the desire of the human to interact with it. If the activity is likely to change the behavior of the animal or place it at increased risk of death, injury, or illness, then it is not an acceptable interaction.

The intended readership of this book is most likely to encounter and have opportunities to interact with marine mammals while boating or swimming from shore. Wildlife watching has become increasingly popular in recent years, leading to the establishment of a National Watchable Wildlife program (see Web site below), and the development of guidelines specific to viewing marine animals. A few basic suggestions can help ensure that these wildlife-viewing experiences are positive for the people as well as for the marine mammals. NOAA Fisheries has presented in one of their brochures and on their Web site[2] a "Marine Mammal and Sea Turtle Viewing Code of Conduct" for the southeastern United States. The five components of this code of conduct are:

(1) Remain a respectful distance from marine mammals and sea turtles. The minimum recommended distances are:

    a. Dolphins, porpoises, seals = 50 m (about 150 feet)

    b. Sea turtles = 50 m (about 150 feet)

    c. Whales = 100 m (about 300 feet)

    d. Right whales = 500 m (about 1,500 feet)

(2) Limit time spent observing marine mammals and sea turtles to half an hour.

(3) Do not encircle or trap marine mammals and sea turtles between watercraft, or between watercraft and shore.

(4) If approached by a marine mammal or sea turtle, put your watercraft's engine into neutral and allow the animal to pass. Any vessel movement should be from the rear of the animal. Federal law prohibits pursuit of marine mammals and sea turtles.

(5) Never feed or attempt to feed marine mammals or sea turtles, in accordance with federal law that prohibits these activities.

Distance and duration criteria are intended to minimize disturbance of marine mammals. Prolonged or repeated exposure to one or more vessels increases the probability of disturbance from underwater noise and proximity. When approaching marine mammals for viewing, it is best to do so slowly and quietly. There is no evidence to support the common notion among some boaters that pounding on the side of a vessel attracts dolphins. Typically, marine mammals seem to be less disturbed by vessels operating at a consistent speed and heading than those that engage in sudden changes in these parameters. Vessels should be positioned such that they remain clear of the path of the animals. Boaters should not pursue the animals, and should not attempt to herd or chase groups of marine mammals; nor should they try to separate individuals from groups or mothers from their young. Viewers should always leave an "escape route" for the animals; this is especially of concern when multiple vessels are present. It is best not to approach a group of marine mammals if another viewing vessel is already present; if more than one vessel is present, the vessels should communicate with each other to ensure that the animals are provided with appropriate options for movement.

Indications of possible disturbance of cetaceans include rapid changes in direction on the surface or underwater, increased swimming speed, prolonged dives, underwater exhalations, explosive surface exhalations ("chuffs"), tail slaps (on the surface of the water), sideways lashing of the tail stock and flukes, and/or interposition of one animal or subgroup between you and the other marine mammals. If you observe any of these behaviors, you should move carefully away from the animals.

Not all interactions between marine mammals and people occur from the decks of private vessels. For example, a whole industry has developed that focuses on providing opportunities to the public to observe bottlenose dolphins in the wild. In the year 2000, there were more than 100 such commercial ventures in Florida.

Patrons of these ventures should not assume that the operators necessarily comply with the laws regulating approaches to marine mammals. A study[3] of commercial dolphin-watching vessels in Pinellas County in 1999–2000 showed that six of seven operators at one time or another violated the Marine Mammal Protection Act; all seven operators violated the dolphin-watching guidelines developed by NOAA Fisheries at least once. The study suggests that the potential for harassment of marine mammals (specifically dolphins) due to commercial ventures is moderate to high.

Thus, we suggest that patrons of commercial dolphin watching operations be attentive to how activities are conducted. If harassment of dolphins or other marine mammals occurs, it would be useful to point out to the operator (perhaps using this book as a guide) that his/her activities are not appropriate. If the inappropriate behaviors continue, it may be prudent to inform the enforcement agencies (federal or state).

Of course, not all viewing of free-ranging marine mammals needs to occur from a boat. There are locations, for example, where hundreds of manatees may be viewed from vantage points at warm-water discharges. Near the Fort Myers Florida Power & Light Company power plant on the Orange River, for example, people can see hundreds of manatees within just a few feet of the shore on a cold winter's day at the so-called Manatee Park; at the same time, park personnel provide information on manatee biology and conservation. A similar situation exists at the Tampa Electric Company plant near Ruskin.

Feeding or otherwise provisioning marine mammals is illegal in the wild, and is contrary to common sense. Providing fish or other objects to dolphins, or plants or freshwater to manatees, can alter their natural behavior, can be harmful to their health, can make them dependent on handouts, and can attract them to potentially dangerous situations with humans. In addition to the health risks posed by providing these animals with inappropriate objects or food items of poor quality (oceanaria must provide food that meets rigorous health standards, comparable with that served to people in restaurants), provisioning reinforces the unnatural behavior of approaching people. In essence, people feeding wild marine mammals are inadvertently conditioning or training them to be attracted to situations that can put them at risk of harm from unaware or malevolent humans, and to beg for food that they don't need and that can sometimes be harmful.

Begging behavior apparently can spread through a dolphin population through observational learning, with potentially tragic results. For example, south of Sarasota Bay, Florida, a four-year-old male calf of a

A benign way to observe and learn about manatees: viewing them at a winter warm-water discharge. Sheri Barton.

begging female bottlenose dolphin was observed begging up to several weeks prior to its death in 2000. He stranded alive but died shortly thereafter, with evidence of several kinds of human interactions. The young dolphin was extremely emaciated, weighing only half of what would be typical for a dolphin of his length and age. He had a fishing hook and line in his stomach, there were scars from line entanglement on his dorsal and pectoral fins, and he had three large, deep, parallel vertical slices on his tail stock, indicative of boat propeller wounds. Though the specific role of begging in the sequence of events that led to this dolphin's demise cannot be determined, it is clear that this animal, a known beggar, was involved in a surprisingly high number of adverse human interactions.

In addition to provisioning, swimming with and touching wild marine mammals are also inappropriate. Federal guidelines prohibit swimming with cetaceans, and limit such activities with manatees to a few areas where "no swim" zones have been established nearby to allow manatees the opportunity to avoid humans. It is our opinion that any attempt to swim with marine mammals has the potential to disturb them, and people should not attempt to swim with these animals under any circumstances in the wild. In the absence of food offerings, most marine mammals (some manatees excepted) are not attracted to human swimmers; in fact they typically move quickly away from humans entering the water nearby, which is evidence that they have been disturbed.

Close proximity to marine mammals, through boating, feeding, or swimming with them, sometimes comes with an associated risk of injury to humans. Large whales have the potential to damage vessels or harm humans while breaching, flipper slapping, and tail slapping, or when startled by vessels passing overhead. Manatees startled by quiet vessels such as canoes or kayaks passing overhead in shallow water have been known to inadvertently capsize such vessels or send their occupants over the side. Bottlenose dolphins conditioned to receive food from people in the wild have been known to bite empty hands reaching to touch the begging animals, and to attack swimmers, inflicting serious injuries requiring medical attention. None of these actions should be taken to mean that these marine mammals are naturally aggressive toward humans—in most cases, the animals are simply responding to unnatural situations created by humans.

Vessel operations are perhaps the most pervasive sources of death, injury, and disturbance of marine mammals. This is especially true for en-

Beggar, a dolphin from south of Sarasota Bay, Florida, has been "trained" by boaters to perform a variety of unnatural behaviors. Randall S. Wells.

Photograph of a dead dolphin calf with a history of begging from humans, with injuries from a boat propeller, line entanglement, and fishing gear ingestion. Nélio B. Barros.

dangered manatees and right whales. About 69 percent of nonnewborn manatee carcasses bear scars from boat collisions; of these, 70 percent bear evidence of multiple boat strikes during their lives, with at least two recovered carcasses showing marks from about 50 strikes. Boats strike even normally nimble bottlenose dolphins on occasion, with about 4 percent of individuals in Sarasota Bay bearing propeller scars. Collisions with marine mammals can be minimized in several ways. There is no substitute for operator vigilance. Continuous visual monitoring of the waters ahead of the boat can go far to avoid collisions. Any pattern on the water's surface that looks different from the surrounding waters, such as changes in ripples, boils, swirls, bubbles, floating objects, etc., can be indicative of a marine mammal in your boat's path. When manatees breathe, they may only show their nostrils above the water's surface, giving little hint of the massive body below.

Compliance with established boat speed zones can also reduce the probability of collision. For example, "manatee zones" are typically established in regions of high manatee use. Slow vessel speeds provide the animals with time to move out of the way of an approaching boat. Recent studies led by Stephanie Nowacek, working with Wells and colleagues, examined responses of manatees to approaching boats. This was accomplished by observing manatees via a video camera suspended from a helium-filled airship tethered 60 m (200 feet) above a small houseboat. Looking down through the water column, we were able to observe manatees continuously, whether at the surface or below. Nearly half of the manatees appeared to respond to any vessels passing within 100 m (about 300 feet), and the intensity of the response increased as the distance to the boat decreased. Typically, responses were initiated when a vessel was at a distance far greater than the horizontal underwater visibility, suggesting the importance of manatee hearing for detecting approaching boats. A common manatee response involves moving from shallow waters such as sea grass meadows or channel edges to the nearest deep water, typically a channel, and this response often brings the manatee into the path of the approaching boat. Thus, slow vessel speeds can provide the animals with the time they need to complete their move to deeper waters, where they can pass safely beneath vessels. Reynolds in *Mysterious Manatees* discusses this issue in some detail.

Vessel operations in shallow waters provide a case of special concern to marine mammals. Both manatees and dolphins use very shallow waters, at times moving through water less than 3 feet (1 m) deep. The manatees use these waters to feed, to rest, or perhaps to avoid the advances of groups of libidinous males. Dolphins often feed on fishes associated with sea grasses in these shallows. Twenty years ago, these waters were essentially free from powerboats, creating a reasonably safe area for marine mammals to conduct their activities. Today, with the advent of personal watercraft, shallow draft flats boats, and airboats, high-speed vessels have access to all of the habitats occupied by marine mammals. In these situations, there is often insufficient water depth to allow the clear passage of vessels over the marine mammals, leading to collisions or extreme behavioral responses. Bottlenose dolphins are about 3 feet (1 m) tall, from belly to dorsal fin tip, and large manatees can approach this height from belly to back. Thus, in waters less than about 6 feet (2 m) deep, there is little chance of a propeller or skeg passing safely over a submerged manatee or dolphin. Using the same overhead video system described above, Nowacek, Wells, and colleagues observed bottlenose dolphins in shallow waters while boats approached, and reported significant heading and swim speed changes as boats approached. A precautionary approach for operating vessels in waters less than 6 feet (2 m) involves moving slowly through the shallow areas. This minimizes the possibility of serious injury, death, and disturbance, and provides a secondary benefit of reducing propeller damage to sea grass meadows.

Fishing gear, both commercial and recreational, can harm marine mammals. Though large commercial gill nets are no longer allowed in inshore Florida waters, they are still a concern in many parts of the ranges of marine mammals. Many bottlenose dolphins die each year in North Carolina, for example, from entanglement in fishing nets. Commercial and recreational crab trap float lines have been responsible for an increasing number of manatee and dolphin injuries and deaths in Florida and elsewhere in the southeastern United States. This problem typically results, in part, from excess float line attached to the trap, more than what is required to reach the surface on a high tide. Marine mammals become entangled in loops of line, resulting in the line cutting into and sometimes severing appendages, or drowning the animal. The potential for these problems can be reduced dramatically by making a conscientious effort to set only as much float line as is absolutely necessary for the float to reach the surface, and/or to stiffen the float line by running it through material such as garden hose, which reduces the possibility of loop formation. In addition, removal of derelict traps and lines from the water helps reduce the possibility that marine mammals or sea turtles may become entangled.

In some parts of the southeastern United States, dolphins have become entangled in crab pot lines as they attempt to tip the pots over and steal the bait. Some intrepid fishermen have placed their bait wells such that dolphins cannot get to the bait; as a result, dolphins in some areas have learned that they cannot benefit from tipping over crab pots and have ceased this dangerous behavior.

Careful use of fishing line and tackle can also reduce marine mammal injuries and deaths. It is not uncommon to recover stranded marine mammals that have masses of monofilament fishing line wrapped around their bodies. Often these balls of line show cuts in many places, indicating that they were cut off a reel and discarded into the water. Unwanted fishing line should be placed in appropriate receptacles where it cannot return to the water. In some cases, fishing line breaks when snagged on obstacles, or when an angler is fighting a fish. Such breaks are clearly unintentional, but even these instances might be reduced by carefully checking fishing line to ensure that it is functioning at full breaking strength, and by replacing line frequently. Similarly, frequent checks of terminal tackle can reduce the possibility that fish will break the line near the end and then be eaten by dolphins along with the hooks, lures, and associated fishing line. We also recommend that fishing be briefly curtailed while dolphins are in the vicinity, to reduce the chance that the dolphins will be attracted to hooked fish, and to eliminate the possibility of foul-hooking the animals.

Everyone can participate in efforts to keep the waters used by Florida's marine mammals clean. Boaters and beach walkers can pick up trash. Ingestion of foreign objects is a source of illness and mortality for marine mammals and sea turtles. In many areas there are annual coastal clean-up programs conducted by volunteers. Reducing chemical inputs into the waters is also important. Pesticides and herbicides applied in yards can make their way as runoff into the tributaries that lead to the waters used by Florida's marine mammals. Spillage of gas and oil is all too frequent an occurrence near Florida docks and ramps. Fertilizers enrich coastal waters, leading to changes in water quality and vegetation and fueling speculation that they might be exacerbating some conditions such as red tides. Reducing or at least controlling application and use of chemicals at home and on the water will improve the quality of the environment in which marine mammals live, and where we recreate or earn our living.

The keys to sharing the world of Florida's marine mammals are simple and few—respect Florida's waters as the homes of these animals, follow protective regulations, and apply common sense to conduct your activities in the best interests of the animals. Not only will these animals have a better chance of surviving and thriving in Florida's waters, but also people using the same waters will benefit from the improved quality of the environment.

Marine Mammal Strandings

Stranded marine mammals have long been curiosities for humans; more than 2000 years ago, Aristotle commented on them. Until early in the last century, most of what we knew about many cetacean species, in particular, came from examination of stranded animals. Each year, about 200–300 whales or dolphins strand on Florida's beaches; an equal number (around 300) of dead manatees is discovered and recovered each year as well in Florida. Most of the cetaceans are beach-cast carcasses, but some are living dolphins and whales. Members of the public are usually the first to encounter these stranded animals, but if appropriate authorities have been contacted a team of experts should soon arrive on the scene to transport the living animal to the nearest rehabilitation facility, or to recover the carcass for a necropsy to attempt to discover the cause of death and to gather information and samples for biological research.

In 1977, a major step was taken to coordinate responses to stranding events on a national level. The U.S. Marine Mammal Stranding Network was formally established as a result of a workshop held in Athens, Georgia. This volunteer network consists of trained individuals (such as animal care experts, scientists, and veterinarians), research and/or educational institutions, and marine mammal facilities located around the coastline of the United States. These individuals and organizations are formally and legally authorized by NOAA Fisheries to investigate reports of strandings, and to respond appropriately, relative to their capabilities. For the species under its jurisdiction, NOAA Fisheries oversees the ad-

Some species, like the pilot whales shown here on a Jacksonville Beach, "mass strand." Randall S. Wells.

ministrative and legal aspects of the network, and a regional scientific coordinator serves as the depository of the data archives. The Marine Mammal Health and Stranding Response Program of NOAA Fisheries provides additional guidance and resources during unusual stranding events. For manatees, such coordination and research are done by the state's Fish and Wildlife Conservation Commission.

People who encounter stranded marine mammals should first understand that they have the potential to do more harm than good, to both the animals and themselves, in the absence of appropriate guidance. The first action taken should be to contact the Florida Fish and Wildlife Conservation Commission Division of Law Enforcement (telephone number: 1-888-404-3922 [404-FWCC]), or local law enforcement agencies. Ask them for instructions about whether or how to respond. In general, it is best for inexperienced people not to handle the animals and to wait for the authorized experts to arrive and direct operations. In the case of a live stranding, some immediate action may be required to stabilize the animal before the responding team can arrive. In this event, carefully follow the instructions provided to you, and be mindful of the fact that even the smaller marine mammals are still very powerful animals that can be very dangerous under dire circumstances such as a stranding. Further, stranded animals may be diseased, and the pathogens they carry may be of concern for your own health. The responding team should be able to evaluate the situation very quickly upon arrival, and will inform you of the risks as well as provide guidance on how you can be of greatest assistance.

chapter 5

Additional Sources of Information

The volume of information about marine mammals has expanded tremendously over the last several decades. Not only is more and better information available, but it is available in many different forms, including scientific journals, books, television and videos, compact discs, and Web sites, and through visits to zoos, aquaria, and oceanaria. An exhaustive list of these resources is beyond the scope of this book, but we will try to point the reader to some of the more pertinent sources for the animals and issues of Florida.

The bibliography section of this book is a good place to start for finding written material. The literature cited in that section provides detailed background information, and most of the references should be easily accessible through libraries or bookstores. Peer-reviewed scientific journals such as *Marine Mammal Science* (published by the Society for Marine Mammalogy; see Web site at *www.marinemammalogy.org/mms.htm*), *Aquatic Mammals* (published by the European Association for Aquatic Mammals; see *www.eaam.org/aquamamm.htm*), *The Journal of Cetacean Research and Management* (published by the International Whaling Commission and available at their Web site at *www.iwcoffice. org,*) and the *Canadian Journal of Zoology* (link can be found at *www. nrc.ca*) offer some of the best and most up-to-date articles on marine mammals; such references are often not available in public libraries, but may be found in college or university libraries, or through the journals' Web sites.

A companion video to this book is available for educational purposes through Mote Marine Laboratory. This 15-minute VHS-format video titled *Human Interactions with Florida's Marine Mammals* is available for the cost of copying, handling, and shipping. This video was produced in 1999 through the support of the Florida Fish and Wildlife Conservation Commission's Florida Marine Research Institute. It presents some of the threats being faced by manatees and bottlenose dolphins in Florida. Some of the footage is derived from the overhead video system described earlier in this book, providing a unique perspective of how these animals respond to some human interactions. Suggestions for how to interact with Florida's marine mammals are also presented. To order this video, send a check for $10 U.S. made payable to "Mote Marine Laboratory" to:

Marine Mammal Video
Center for Marine Mammal and Sea Turtle Research
Mote Marine Laboratory
1600 Ken Thompson Parkway
Sarasota, Florida 34236 USA

This video has the merits of being relatively up to date, focused on Florida's marine mammals, and attentive to the effects of human interactions on the animals. There are other videos as well that have some of the same attributes; these include, but are not limited to the following: *Silent Sirens*[1] (a somewhat dated video that deals with still-present conservation issues for manatees in Florida), *Mammals of the Sea*[2] (deals with marine mammal interactions with people around the United States), and the NOVA film *The Private Lives of Dolphins*[3] (focuses on research and conservation activities for bottlenose dolphins in Florida and Australia).

Web sites provide access to a great deal of information, but because the information outside of scientific journals is not peer reviewed, one must exercise caution before accepting some of the available information as fact. Among the more useful Web sites we have found are the following:

There are some good sites that provide guidelines for viewing wildlife generally, or manatees specifically. The National Watchable Wildlife program provides numerous tips about how to minimize human impacts while observing a variety of wildlife at *www.watchablewildlife.org/*

The Florida Fish and Wildlife Conservation Commission and the Save the Manatee Club provide some manatee viewing guidelines at *www.floridaconservation.org/psm/manatee/guide.htm* and *www.savethemanatee.org/Tips.htm*

NOAA Fisheries provides the following site for guidance specifically for marine mammal viewing. In addition, this Office of Protected Resources site provides updates on federal management activities related to marine mammals: *www.nmfs.noaa.gov/prot_res/MMWatch/MMViewing.html*

The U.S. Geological Survey sponsors one of the longest-running manatee research programs, based in Gainesville, Florida: *www.fcsc.usgs.gov/Manatees/manatees.html*

The U.S. Fish and Wildlife Service has an office in Jacksonville that coordinates management activities for a number of species (including the West Indian manatee) under that agency's jurisdiction. Information regarding manatees is available at *www.ecos.fws.gov/servlet/SpeciesProfile?spcode=A007*

The State of Florida's manatee research program and current management activities are described at *www.floridamarine.org*

Also, the Bureau of Protected Species Management for the State has the following site: *www.floridaconservation.org/psm/*

The Society for Marine Mammalogy offers the following site as a source for its quarterly newsletter, including information on marine mammal issues, as well as an online brochure on "Strategies for Pursuing a Career in Marine Mammalogy": *www.marinemammalogy.org/*

Harbor Branch Oceanographic Institution administers a "Protect Wild Dolphins" program funded by Florida dolphin license tag revenues. This program supports HBOI dolphin research and rehabilitation programs, as well as some external research programs in the State of Florida: *www.protectwilddolphins.org/info.html*

Mote Marine Laboratory's marine mammal research and conservation programs are described on their Web site: *www.mote.org*

The Chicago Zoological Society's Brookfield Zoo Web site provides information on its long-term dolphin research program in Sarasota Bay, Florida, as well as an interactive program, "Dolphins in Depth," designed to provide children with a better understanding of dolphins and dolphin research: *www.brookfieldzoo.org* and *www.sarasotadolphin.org*

The Hubbs SeaWorld Research Institute (HSWRI) has its headquarters in California, but also has an office associated with SeaWorld in Orlando. The HSWRI in Florida conducts a range of studies of cetacean biology and habitat use, focusing on bottlenose dolphins in the Indian River Lagoon. In addition, research staff have initiated some recent work on captive manatees. More information can be found at *www.hswri.org*

The Disney Wildlife Conservation Fund has supported a wide range of studies, including several dealing with marine mammals in Florida. The fund "helps ensure the survival of wildlife and wild places in all their beauty and diversity." Details and lists of organizations supported by the fund may be found at *www.gm-unccd.org/FIELD/Private/Disney/ Wdgrants.htm* and at *disney.go.com/disneyhand/environmentality/dwcf_ organizations.html*

There are many conservation organizations that have become involved in "the manatee issue." It is beyond the scope of this book to list them all, and it should be noted that the various organizations do not necessarily have exactly the same perspective on issues. We note the Save the Manatee Club here, not necessarily as an endorsement, but rather to reflect its efforts for many years as an advocacy group for manatee protection: *www.savethemanatee.org*

Numerous opportunities exist in Florida for members of the public to observe and learn about marine mammals from shore, from commercial vessels, or at facilities holding captive marine mammals. For example, the TECO power plant at Apollo Beach, Florida, provides an overlook that offers opportunities to view many manatees during cold months when the animals return to take advantage of the warm water effluent. Captive manatees can be observed at Mote Marine Laboratory in Sarasota, Lowry Park Zoo in Tampa, Bishop Planetarium in Bradenton, Miami Seaquarium, EPCOT's Living Seas in Orlando, and SeaWorld Florida in Orlando. Captive dolphins can be seen at nearly a dozen facilities in Florida; many of these offer interactive programs to those so inclined. Dolphin- or manatee-watching tours are available from many coastal sites.

chapter 6

For the Concerned Citizen

People of all ages and all walks of life have asked how they can become involved in meaningful ways in helping to promote research or conservation of marine mammals. In reality, there are a number of ways concerned citizens can make a difference.

One way is simply to become and stay informed regarding issues and to voice your feelings and concerns to elected officials. A number of legislators at the federal and state levels have made a tremendous difference by activities such as promoting protective legislation or ensuring that appropriations for research and conservation activities are adequate. Of course, elected officials, like everybody, have their own values and opinions, and not all of them are anxious to support conservation or scientific research on marine mammals or other species. But members of Congress and other elected decision makers also attempt to reflect the opinions of the people who put them in office in the first place. Well-articulated, rational, informed, and balanced opinions to elected officials can make a real difference. Some useful Web sites that provide links to elected representatives in the Florida legislature, to regional councils, or to relevant statutes include: *www.leg.state.fl.us, www.myflorida.com/portal.government,* and *www.flsenate.gov/statutes.* Most counties have individual Web pages listing their commissioners and laws.

But what should the layperson believe when there are often widely divergent points of view and considerable misinformation about many issues? Herein lies the crux of an enormous problem. Many members of the media (certainly not all!) develop stories about issues, the more controversial the better. In such cases, interviews with individuals who seek to promote common ground among parties may not be deemed newsworthy or be reflected in printed articles; instead, articles may reflect more spirited and polarized quotations.

The reality is that for most issues there is extensive common ground, but certain individuals on all sides may fan the flames by focusing on what they may perceive as irreconcilable differences, rather than on building partnerships and working as cooperatively as possible. These people may exaggerate or distort information to attempt to support their own points of view as strongly as possible. Such individuals represent conservation interests as well as a variety of economic enterprises. This topic is discussed at some length in Reynolds's recent book, *Mysterious Manatees.*

Scientists themselves bear a lot of the blame for the lack of factual information on many topics written for the lay public. Consider the professional incentives for promotion and fame in scientific fields: generally, scientists are rewarded for writing technical papers for their peers. Writing for the lay public is viewed by many scientists and administrators not simply as something that carries no rewards (and hence provides no motivation) but actually as an activity to be avoided because it detracts from the development of "real publications." Until "the system" changes to induce scientists to become good communicators of their work to the general public, there will be unfortunate voids in what people are able to perceive about crucial issues.

Nonetheless, we hope people will take the time to read and become informed about all sides of issues as thoroughly as possible. In chapter 5 we provide a number of resources that, we believe, offer factual and balanced perspectives. And, as a rule, we suggest trusting the "golden mean." Few issues in life are black and white.

Environmental Advocacy Groups

Many people join or wish to join environmental advocacy groups in an effort to help save particular species or habitats. There are, to be sure, a number of extremely dedicated groups that have successfully promoted effective conservation programs. There are also some organizations that use most of their donated money to support salaries for their own administrators. Just because a group claims to be dedicated to a cause doesn't mean that it actually is! We both belong to conservation organizations ourselves, and we believe such groups can accomplish an enormous amount. However, before you join and contribute to such a group, we recommend you do some careful homework. Find out what the goals and objectives of the organization are; assess what the group has done to date; determine whether the group seems to fit your own goals, be they moderate or more extreme; and ask what percentage of the money you donate goes to issues and what percentage goes to salaries, offices, and other things. Doing a little homework will allow you to support activities and issues dear to your heart—and to help make a difference.

Careers in Marine Mammal Science and Conservation

The best single source of information on this topic (as noted also in chapter 5) is found at the Web site for the international Society for Marine Mammalogy (SMM) (*www.marinemammalogy.org/*). There, interested people can find a booklet (specifically at *www.marinemammalogy.org/strat.htm*) that provides considerable information on careers in this field.

We won't repeat all that is contained in the SMM career guide. But we shall venture an opinion. Being well meaning is great, but being informed and careful with facts is better. There are many instances in which poor science or poor interpretation of science has caused a great deal more harm to a conservation issue than would have been the case if there were no scientific information at all. The same holds true for some well-intended but scientifically off-base conservation efforts; they caused more harm than good because people just didn't do their homework.

Becoming a scientist or conservationist truly requires more than simply caring and dedication. It requires rigor, professionalism, and scientific honesty and integrity when collecting and presenting factual information. If that isn't something that you are willing to do, then make marine mammals your avocation (where you can still do a lot) rather than your vocation.

Internships and Volunteerism

For the individual who wishes to experience marine mammals and to assist in their care, scientific research, or conservation, there are varied and extensive opportunities to become involved. A rather comprehensive listing of opportunities and links to other Web pages has been developed by University of South Florida and appears at *ompl.marine.usf.edu/mmsg/ marinemammallinks.htm*. For a couple of specific examples, at Mote Marine Laboratory, the Center for Marine Mammal and Sea Turtle Research benefits tremendously from the efforts of more than 40 undergraduate volunteer interns each year. Hundreds of volunteers have been trained to assist with the care of stranded cetaceans at Mote's Dolphin and Whale Hospital. In addition, more than 60 volunteers from the general public participate in observational field studies of marine mammals each year at Mote Marine Laboratory (and at many other locations around the world as well) through Earthwatch Institute (*www.earthwatch.org/*), an organization based in Maynard, Mass., that matches environmentally oriented people with projects in need of their assistance for two weeks at a time (telephone number: 800-776-0188).

Who needs volunteers? Lots of places do. Research laboratories, marine zoological parks, marine mammal rehabilitation facilities, academic research programs, and museums are just a few of the places that can use the help of interested and reliable people.

Other Ways to Help

One of the ways that members of the public can get involved in marine mammal conservation is to report violations of the regulations protecting these animals. Law enforcement agents deployed in the area can be dispatched via radio to scenes of violations. The Florida Fish and Wildlife Conservation Commission's Law Enforcement Division (formerly Florida Marine Patrol) can be contacted by telephone toll-free at: 1-888-404-3922 (*www.floridaconservation.org/law/*). NOAA Fisheries Law Enforcement can be contacted at the regional office in St. Petersburg at:

1-727-570-5344, toll-free at 800-853-1964 or on the Web (*www.nmfs. noaa.gov/ole/fen.html*).

A Final Thought

A children's book titled *What If Everybody Did That?* by Ellen Javernich conveys an interesting message that adults might heed. Suppose one person threw some trash out of a car window; that wouldn't really create much of a problem. But suppose everybody did it; then the world would get covered in trash. Suppose one person let a faucet run all day; the world wouldn't go dry. But, again, suppose everybody did it . . . You get the idea.

In ecology we call the problem illustrated by such examples a problem of scale. If something happens at a tiny scale, a species or an ecosystem may be able to survive just fine. But if the problem exists on a grand scale—in other words, if everybody does it—then the species or the system might collapse. That's the problem humans face on so many ecological and other fronts today. That's why we face regulations in terms of the numbers and sizes of the fish we can catch; that's why we are prohibited from developing certain locations; and that's why behaving in a respectful manner to marine mammals and other species is necessary if we want them to be around into the future.

If you were to disrupt the day of a dolphin or a manatee, that event might not be critical. But if that same disruption were to occur 100 times every day year-round, it would be a different story. We may want to recall the simple but direct message of *What If Everybody Did That?* as we gauge the footprint we leave behind.

Notes

Chapter 1. People and Marine Mammals in Florida

1. From the video *Silent Sirens,* produced by the Florida Audubon Society, Maitland, 1980.

2. See, for example, Alpers, *Dolphins: The Myth and the Mammal.*

3. Lavigne, Scheffer, and Kellert, "The evolution of North American attitudes toward marine mammals," 40.

Chapter 2. Natural History of Florida's Marine Mammals

1. The word "teach" is in quotations because it is quite likely that female manatees do not actively teach their offspring. Rather, the young manatees may learn simply by following and imitating their mothers.

2. Otto et al., "Paving our way to water shortages: how sprawl aggravates drought," 4–6.

3. See Reynolds, Wells, and Eide, *The Bottlenose Dolphin: Biology and Conservation,* and Pringle and Wells, *Dolphin Man: Exploring the World of Dolphins.*

4. Waring, Quintal, and Swartz, "U.S. Atlantic and Gulf of Mexico marine mammal stock assessments."

5. Wells, Hofmann, and Moors, "Entanglement and mortality of bottlenose dolphins in recreational fishing gear in Florida."

6. Wells and Scott, "Seasonal incidence of boat strikes on bottlenose dolphins near Sarasota, Florida."

7. Nowacek, Wells, and Solow, "The effects of boat traffic on bottlenose dolphins in Sarasota Bay, Florida."

8. Leatherwood and Reeves, "Bottlenose dolphin and other toothed cetaceans," Table 18.6, 374, and Scott, "Management-oriented research on bottlenose dolphins," Table 1, 624.

9. Norris et al., *The Hawaiian Spinner Dolphin.*

10. Located on the record album *Whales and Nightingales,* Elektra Records, New York.

11. Weight-specific metabolism is a term that describes how many calories an animal requires per unit of body weight (say per pound of body weight). Larger animals, perhaps a little counterintuitively, need fewer calories per unit of body weight than do smaller animals. For example, a human eats far more than a mouse, but the mouse has a higher weight-specific metabolic rate. Readers who have ever kept pet mice or gerbils already have a feeling for this, since they know that their pets will starve if left unfed for many hours, whereas the average adult human can exist (albeit uncomfortably) without food for days.

Chapter 3. Threats and Protection

1. Note that subsistence hunting of marine mammals, including certain whale species, is authorized for Native Alaskans and the Makah tribe in Washington.

2. See Reynolds, *Mysterious Manatees.*

3. *Year of the Ocean Discussion Papers,* iii–v.

4. For an up-to-date and thorough assessment of the many effects of fishing (and overfishing) in the United States, we recommend Dayton, Thrush, and Coleman, *Ecological Effects of Fishing in Marine Ecosystems of the United States.*

5. Klesius, "The State of the Planet."

6. Baur, Bean, and Gosliner, "The laws governing marine mammal conservation in the United States," 49.

7. The issue of burden of proof and its use and misuse is dealt with well by Dayton, "Reversal of the burden of proof in fisheries management."

8. The case in question is *Strong v. United States.* It is described by Baur et al., "The laws governing marine mammal conservation in the United States," and in a number of annual reports to Congress by the U.S. Marine Mammal Commission.

9. Swim-with-the-dolphin programs have been and continue to be quite controversial. Some advocates of such programs have even claimed that medical benefits exist to some individuals who participate, whereas others indicate that the data supporting such claims are flawed. For a discussion of the programs, their putative ben-

efits and problems, and references dealing with the topic, see Reynolds, Wells, and Eide, *The Bottlenose Dolphin: Biology and Conservation.*

10. It is worth noting that different swim-with-the-dolphin programs at public display facilities exert different levels of control over the interactions between the humans and the dolphins. Programs that exert less control pose greater risks to both the people and the dolphins than do more controlled interactions. This topic is considered in detail by Samuels and Spradlin, "Behavioral study of bottlenose dolphins in swim-with-the-dolphin programs," and more generally by Reynolds, Wells, and Eide, *The Bottlenose Dolphin: Biology and Conservation.*

11. Thankfully, the agency has not taken the same position with other species under its jurisdiction. Swimming with polar bears, for example, is not something to be encouraged!

12. Reynolds, "Efforts to conserve the manatees," 287.

Chapter 4. Guidelines for Human Interaction with Mammals

1. Although "guidelines" may not always have the force of law, they are designed to help the public and commercial operators avoid situations that could constitute harassment.

2. Available at *www.nmfs.noaa.gov/prot_res/MMWatch/MMViewing.html*

3. Herrington, "Adherence to the Marine Mammal Protection Act." Readers should note that this report is not peer reviewed or published. It is a senior thesis, available through the Eckerd College (St. Petersburg, Fla.) library.

Chapter 5. Additional Sources of Information

1. *Silent Sirens*, produced by the Florida Audubon Society, Maitland, 1980.

2. *Mammals of the Sea,* produced by Sea Grant at Oregon State University, Corvallis, 1980.

3. *The Private Lives of Dolphins,* produced by WGBH Educational Foundation, Boston, and MDTV Productions, 1992.

Bibliography

Alpers, A. *Dolphins: The Myth and the Mammal.* Cambridge, Mass.: Riverside Press, 1961.

Baur, D. C., M. J. Bean, and M. L. Gosliner. "The laws governing marine mammal conservation in the United States." 48–86. In J. R. Twiss Jr. and R. R. Reeves, eds., *Conservation and Management of Marine Mammals.* Washington, D.C.: Smithsonian Institution Press, 1999.

Dayton, P. K. "Reversal of the burden of proof in fisheries management." *Science* 279 (1998): 821–22.

Dayton, P. K., S. Thrush, and F. C. Coleman. *Ecological Effects of Fishing in Marine Ecosystems of the United States.* Arlington, Va.: Pew Oceans Commission, 2002.

Domning, D. P. "Why save the manatee?" 167–73. *In* J. E. Reynolds III and D. K. Odell, *Manatees and Dugongs.* New York: Facts on File, 1991.

Glaser, K., and J. E. Reynolds III. *Mysterious Manatees.* Gainesville: University Press of Florida, 2003.

Herrington, K. L. "Adherence to the Marine Mammal Protection Act by dolphin-watching companies in Pinellas County, Florida." St. Petersburg, Fla.: senior thesis, Eckerd College, 2000.

Javernich, E. *What If Everybody Did That?* Chicago: Children's Press, Scholastic Library Publishing, 1990.

Jefferson, T. A., S. Leatherwood, and M. A. Webber. *Marine Mammals of the World.* Rome: United Nations Environment Programme, Food and Agriculture Organization of the United Nations, 1993.

Klesius, M. "The state of the planet." *National Geographic* 202 (Sept. 2002): 102–15.

Lavigne, D. M., V. B. Scheffer, and S. R. Kellert. "The evolution of North American attitudes toward marine mammals," 10–47. *In* J. R. Twiss Jr. and R. R. Reeves, eds., *Conservation and Management of Marine Mammals*. Washington, D.C.: Smithsonian Institution Press, 1999.

Leatherwood, S., and R. R. Reeves. "Bottlenose dolphin (*Tursiops truncatus*) and other toothed cetaceans," 369–414. *In* J. A. Chapman and G. A. Feldhamer, eds., *Wild Mammals of North America: Biology, Management, and Economics*. Baltimore: Johns Hopkins University Press, 1982.

———. *The Sierra Club Handbook of Whales and Dolphins*. San Francisco: Sierra Club Books, 1983.

Marine Mammal Commission. *Annual Report to Congress 2001*. Washington, D.C., 2002.

Norris, K. S., B. Würsig, R. S. Wells, and M. Würsig. *The Hawaiian Spinner Dolphin*. Berkeley: University of California Press, 1994.

Nowacek, S. M., R. S. Wells, and A. R. Solow. "The effects of boat traffic on bottlenose dolphins, *Tursiops truncatus*, in Sarasota Bay, Florida." *Marine Mammal Science* 17 (2001): 673–88.

Otto, B., K. Ransel, J. Todd, D. Lovaas, H. Stutzman, and J. Bailey. "Paving our way to water shortages: how sprawl aggravates the effects of drought." Unpublished report by American Rivers, National Resources Defense Council, and Smart Growth America, 2002. See Web site: <*www.americanrivers.org*>.

Powell, J. *Manatees*. Stillwater, Minn.: Voyageur Press, 2002.

Pringle, L., and R. S. Wells. *Dolphin Man: Exploring the World of Dolphins*. Honesdale, Pa.: Boyds Mills Press, 2002.

Reeves, R. R., B. S. Stewart, P. J. Clapham, and J. A. Powell. *National Audubon Society Guide to Marine Mammals of the World*. New York: Alfred A. Knopf, 2002.

Reeves, R. R., B. S. Stewart, and S. Leatherwood. *The Sierra Club Handbook of Seals and Sirenians*. San Francisco: Sierra Club Books, 1992.

Reynolds, J. E., III. "Efforts to conserve the manatees," 267–95. In J. R. Twiss Jr. and R. R. Reeves, eds., *Conservation and Management of Marine Mammals*. Washington, D.C.: Smithsonian Institution Press, 1999.

Reynolds, J. E., III, and D. K. Odell. *Manatees and Dugongs*. New York: Facts on File, 1991.

Reynolds, J. E., III, and S. A. Rommel, eds. *Biology of Marine Mammals*. Washington, D.C.: Smithsonian Institution Press, 1999.

Reynolds, J. E., III, R. S. Wells, and S. D. Eide. *The Bottlenose Dolphin: Biology and Conservation.* Gainesville: University Press of Florida, 2000.

Rice, D. W. *Marine Mammals of the World: Systematics and Distribution.* Lawrence, Kans.: Society for Marine Mammalogy, Special Publication 4, 1998.

Ripple, J. *Manatees and Dugongs of the World.* Stillwater, Minn.: Voyageur Press, 1999.

Samuels, A., and T. Spradlin. "Quantitative behavioral study of bottlenose dolphins in swim-with-the-dolphin programs in the United States." *Marine Mammal Science* 11(4) (1995): 520–44.

Scott, G. P. "Management-oriented research on bottlenose dolphins by the Southeast Fisheries Center," 623–39. *In* S. Leatherwood and R. R. Reeves, eds., *The Bottlenose Dolphin.* San Diego: Academic Press, 1990.

Twiss, J. R., Jr., and R. R. Reeves, eds. *Conservation and Management of Marine Mammals.* Washington, D.C.: Smithsonian Institution Press, 1999.

Waring, G. T., J. M. Quintal, and S. L. Swartz, eds. "U.S. Atlantic and Gulf of Mexico marine mammal stock assessments—2001." NOAA Technical Memorandum NMFS-NE-168. 2001. Up-to-date stock assessments for most marine mammal species in the southeastern United States appear at the following Web site: <*www.nefsc.noaa.gov/psb/assesspdfs.htm*>

Wells, R. S., S. Hofmann, and T. L. Moors. "Entanglement and mortality of bottlenose dolphins (*Tursiops truncatus*) in recreational fishing gear in Florida." *Fishery Bulletin* 96 (1998): 647–50.

Wells, R. S. and M. D. Scott. "Seasonal incidence of boat strikes on bottlenose dolphins near Sarasota, Florida." *Marine Mammal Science* 13 (1997): 475–80.

Würsig, B., T. A. Jefferson, and D. J. Schmidly. *The Marine Mammals of the Gulf of Mexico.* College Station: Texas A&M University Press, 2000.

Year of the Ocean Discussion Papers. Washington, D.C.: Office of the Chief Scientist, NOAA, 1998.

Index

Haulouts, manatee, 9, 23
Heavy metals, 44, 90
Herring, 49
Hubbs Sea World Research Institute (HSWRI), 124
Human Interactions with Florida's Marine Mammals, 122
Humans: appreciation of marine mammals, 10–11 (*see also* Tourism); coastal population in Florida, 90, 99 (*see also* Coastal development); coastal population in U.S., 92; guidelines for interaction with marine mammals, 104–20, 135 n.1; injury by marine mammals, 112; mortality from boat accidents, 91; perception of marine mammals, 11, 13, 104, 106; population of Florida, 2; rescued by dolphins, 38; at a stranding site, 119–20
Hunting, subsistence, 85, 95, 105

Indicator species, 6
Information resources: books, 3, 7, 86, 131 (*see also Mysterious Manatees*); journals, 121–22; National Environmental Policy Act chapter, 100; stranding hotline, 119; videos, 9, 122–23; violation hotline, 130; web sites, 121–22, 123–25, 127, 129, 130, 131
Intelligence, 10, 33, 133 n.1
Internships, 129–30

Jack, 49
Journals, 121–22
Juveniles, social groups, 37

"Kerplunking," 39
Kogia breviceps: abundance, 52–53; "Ami," 54; distribution and ranging patterns, 52; mortality factors and threats, 54; physical description, 50–52; social and other behavior, 53–54
Kogia sima: abundance, 52–53; distribution and ranging patterns, 52; mortality factors and threats, 54; physical description, 50, 52; social and other behavior, 53–54
Krill, 60, 84

Lactation: bottlenose dolphin, 29, 44–45; humpback whale, 82; maternal transfer of contaminants, 44–45
Lagenodelphis hosei, 86
Lead, 44
Legislation. *See* Regulations
Lice, whale, 57
Lips: manatee, 18, 23; pygmy killer whale, 70; right whale, 4
Local Government Comprehensive Planning and Land Regulation Act of 1985, 101
Lowry Park Zoo, 125
Lungs, 6

Majorra, 49
Makah tribe, 95
Male pair-bonds, 37, 44, 49
Mammary glands, 6. *See also* Lactation
Management. *See* Policy; Wildlife management
Manatee: Florida (*see Trichechus manatus latirostris*); West Indian, 123
Manatee Park, 110
Manatee Sanctuary Act, 100
"Manatee zones." *See* Boats, speed zones
Mangrove forests, 43, 90
Marine Mammal Health and Stranding Response Program, 119
Marine mammals: characteristics and need for conservation, 12–13; definition, 3–7; guidelines for interaction with, 104–20, 135 n.1; human perception of, 11, 13, 104, 106; as indicator species, 6; injury to humans by, 112; new species, 6, 30, 61, 71; symbolism of, 10, 11
Mass strandings. *See* Strandings
Maternal behavior: Atlantic spotted dolphin, 49; "baby-sitting," 37; bottlenose dolphin, 35; manatee, 19, 133 n.1; right whale, 59
Mating herds, 21
Megaptera novaeangliae: abundance, 84–85; anatomy, 82; distribution and ranging patterns, 84; food and feeding, 82; physical description, 81–84
Mercury, 44, 90
Mesoplodon spp., 71–76, 77

Policy: burden of proof approach, 94; precautionary principle, 106; proactive approach, 88, 99–100; stewardship approach, 10. *See also* Wildlife management

Pollution. *See* Environmental contaminants

Polychlorinated biphenyls (PCB), 44

Porpoise(s): guidelines for interaction, 108; harbor (*see Phocoena phocoena*)

Power plants: Florida Power & Light Company, 27, 110; TECO, 125; warm effluent from, 21–22, 26, 110, 111, 125

Precautionary principle, 106

Predator-prey relationships: Atlantic spotted dolphin, 49; bottlenose dolphin, 34, 38–39, 40–41; "counter shading" camouflage, 50; feeding behavior, 39, 49, 60

Pseudorca crassidens: abundance, 69; distribution and ranging patterns, 69; physical description, 66, 67, 69

Public awareness and participation: coastal cleanup, 116–17; education about regulations, 106–7; environmental advocacy groups, 128; internships, 129–30; motivation, 93, 102; promotion of legislation, 126–27; report of violations, 130–31; volunteerism, 118, 129–30

Rafting, 53

Razor fish, 49

Red tide, 26, 89, 90, 117

Regulations: enforcement, 97, 98, 107, 110, 130–31; federal (*see* U.S. Endangered Species Act of 1973; U.S. Marine Mammal Protection Act of 1972); Florida state, 100–101; jurisdictional issues, 96, 98–99, 101–2; promotion of, 126–27; public education, 106–7

Rehabilitation facilities, 118, 124

Reproductive behavior. *See* Behavior, reproductive

Reproductive organs: bottlenose dolphin, 5, 29; manatee, 5, 19; right whale, 59

Research: capture for, 44, 91–92; communication of science to nonscientists, 127–28; identification by callosities, 57; identification by fin markings, 30; identification by fluke patterns, 82, 83, 84; necropsy, 25, 26, 118; physiological or biomedical, 10; politics

of academia, 127; in science-based decision making, 94; tags and transmitters for monitoring, 17, 21, 91; web sites, 123, 124

Resources. *See* Information resources

Respiration. *See* Breathing

Resting behavior, 53, 81

Rostrum (beak): Atlantic spotted dolphin, 45; bottlenose dolphin, 28; clymene dolphin, 61–62; goosebeak whale, 77; rough-toothed dolphin, 64; spinner dolphin, 63

Sand lance, 84

Save the Manatee Club, 123, 125

Sea grass beds, 23, 38, 43, 93, 115

Seal(s): Caribbean monk, 9; earless, 85; elephant, 10; fur, 85; gray (*see Halichoerus grypus*); guidelines for interaction, 108; harbor (*see Phoca vitulina*); harp (*see Phoca groenlandica*); hooded (*see Cystophora cristata*); hunting of, 89; true, 85

Sea lion(s): California (*see Zalophus californianus*); physical description, 85

Sea turtles: boat strike of, 42; guidelines for interaction, 108; ingestion of trash, 117; red tide mortality, 90; responsible agency, 98

SeaWorld facilities, 124, 125

Shark(s): bull, 40; "cookie cutter," 49, 54, 77; dusky, 40; nurse, 49; similarities to pygmy sperm whale, 50; tiger, 40

Ships. *See* Boats; Boat strike

Sirenians, 3, 9

"Skim-feeding," 60

Social behavior: bottlenose dolphin, 33–38, 44; "fission-fusion," 36; male pair-bonds, 37, 44, 49; manatee, 19–22; right whale, 59; short-finned pilot whale, 68; sperm whale, 80; and strandings, 68

Society for Marine Mammalogy, 124

Sounds by marine mammals. *See* Vocalization

Speed zones. *See* Boats, speed zones

Spot, 38

Springs, natural: and human overuse of aquifer, 26, 27; impact of tourism, 27–28; manatee use of, 21, 26

Squid, 38, 49, 54, 72

State of Florida, 124

Stenella attenuata, 45, 46, 86

Stenella clymene: abundance, 62; anatomy, 45; distribution and ranging patterns, 62; physical description, 61–62

Stenella coeruleoalba, 86

Stenella frontalis: abundance, 48; anatomy, 45; distribution and ranging patterns, 46–48; food and feeding, 49; mortality factors, 49; physical description, 45–46; social and other behavior, 20, 48–49

Stenella longirostris: abundance, 64; anatomy, 45; distribution and ranging patterns, 63–64; physical description, 62–63; social behavior, 20; taxonomy, 61

Steno bredanensis: abundance, 65; distribution and ranging patterns, 64–65; physical description, 64

Stewardship, 10

Stingray, 41

Stock, as management unit, 33

Strandings: annual number in Florida, 118; beaked whale, 73, 74; bottlenose dolphin, 30; clymene dolphin, 62; with entanglement, 116; goosebeak whale, 77; manatee, 118, 119; overview, 118–20; pygmy and dwarf sperm whale, 52, 54; rough-toothed dolphin, 65; short-finned pilot whale, 68, 119; temporary, to capture fish, 30; unknown cause of phenomena, 54, 68, 74; who to call, 119

Stress, 27, 109

"Surfing," 35

Sustainable populations, 94

Swimming: bottlenose dolphin, 35, 43; humpback whale, 84; manatee, 19, 25; pygmy and dwarf sperm whale, 53; right whale, 58, 60; streamlined body plan, 6. *See also* Breaching

Swim-with-the-dolphin programs, 96–97, 134–35 nn.9, 10

Tampa Electric Company (TECO), 110, 125. *See also* Power plants, warm effluent from

Teeth: beaked whale, 72, 74, 75, 76; bottlenose dolphin, 39; clymene dolphin, 61; goosebeak whale, 76–77; manatee, 18–19; pygmy and dwarf sperm whale, 52, 54; rough-toothed dolphin, 64; sperm whale, 79

Temperature homeostasis, 6

Tourism: ecotourism, 2; illegal harassment of dolphins, 43, 91, 95, 97, 112, 134 n.8; impact on manatees, 27–28; importance of common sense, 107, 117; number of tourists in Florida, 2; swim-with-the-dolphin programs, 96–97, 134–35 nn.9, 10; wildlife watching (*see* Wildlife watching)

Toxins. *See* Environmental contaminants

Trichechus manatus latirostris: abundance, 19–20; anatomy, 4, 5, 18–19, 23; "Beau," 21; calves, 18, 20; "Chessie," 19; distribution and ranging patterns, 2, 19; food and feeding, 22–23; four subpopulations, 19–20; lifespan, 25; management agencies, 96; mortality factors and threats, 24, 25–28, 42, 90, 114, 116; physical description, 5, 16; social and other behavior, 20–22; State Marine Mammal of Florida, 9; tagged, 17, 21; watching sites, 110, 111, 125

Tursiops aduncus, 30

Tursiops truncatus: abundance, 32–33; anatomy, 4, 5, 28; cognitive ability, 33; distribution and ranging patterns, 30–32; "Echo," 31; food and feeding, 36, 38–39, 43; lifespan, 30; "Misha," 31; mortality factors and threats, 39–45, 114, 116; physical description, 5, 28–29, 30; predator-prey relationships, 34, 38–39, 40–41; social and other behavior, 33–38, 44; sounds produced by, 34; swimming and diving, 35

Turtles. *See* Sea turtles

Urban sprawl. *See* Coastal development

U.S. Animal and Plant Health Inspection Service, 96, 97

U.S. Congress, reauthorization of legislation, 99

U.S. Department of Commerce. *See* NOAA Fisheries

U.S. Department of Homeland Security, 96

U.S. Department of the Interior. *See* U.S. Fish and Wildlife Service; U.S. Geological Survey

U.S. Endangered Species Act of 1973 (ESA): collection for research purposes, 91; critical habitats under, 58; enforcement, 98, 130–31;

John E. Reynolds III serves as chairman of the United States Marine Mammal Commission, a position to which he was appointed in 1991 by President George Bush. He is also Manatee Research Program manager at Mote Marine Laboratory in Sarasota, Florida, and adjunct professor of marine science and biology at Eckerd College in St. Petersburg, Florida. In addition, he is the co-chair of the Sirenian Specialist Group for the International Union for the Conservation of Nature and Natural Resources. He is coeditor of *Biology of Marine Mammals,* and coauthor of *Manatees and Dugongs, The Bottlenose Dolphin: Biology and Conservation* (UPF, 2000), and *Mysterious Manatees* (UPF, 2003).

Randall S. Wells is a behavioral ecologist with the Conservation Biology Department of the Chicago Zoological Society and adjunct associate professor of ocean sciences at the University of California, Santa Cruz. He also serves as director of the Center for Marine Mammal and Sea Turtle Research at Mote Marine Laboratory, Sarasota, Florida, where he conducts the world's longest running study of wild dolphins. He has worked with a variety of dolphin and whale species, as well as with manatees. He is coauthor of *The Bottlenose Dolphin: Biology and Conservation* (UPF, 2000), *The Hawaiian Spinner Dolphin* (1994), and *Dolphin Man: Exploring the World of Dolphins* (2002).

University Press of Florida
Books of Related Interest